Defiance
In Defense of American
Democracy

(The 'Short' Edition)

Books by
Ivan Lee Weir

The Ida Mae and Oscar Taylor Blackburn
Bookplate Collection
With Natalie Alicia Weir
Privately Printed, 2015

Blackburnes at the Crossroads of History
2018

Stories for My Daughter
Autobiographical Sketches
2021

Murder at Coffee Pot Landing
A Novel of Existential Choices
2023

The Phantom Djinn
A Novel of Afghanistan
2023

The Riverwalk Child
An Art Theft Mystery
2024

Bison River Madam
A novel of Valley Intrigues
2025

Defiance
In Defense of American Democracy

by

Ivan Lee Weir

Published in the United States as an imprint of Writing Ghost Books.

ISBN (soft cover) 9798288184086

First Edition August 2025

Dedication

To the Defenders of Democracy
Whose Message and Persistence
In the End Will be Validated

List of Essays

Preface

It was with a sense of impending disaster I watched the election of November 5, 2024, return Donald J. Trump to the Presidency of the United States. This, I thought, was worse than Nixon's return to the White House because at least Richard Nixon demonstrated a propensity to employ intelligent people to help guide him. It was hard for me to believe from the enthusiasm that surrounded the Kamala Harris campaign that such a despicable person as Donald Trump could garner enough votes to defeat her. Trump's record—denial of Covid 19, distrust of medical scientists and even disparagement of the doctors who saved his life, felonies, scandals and illegal handling of government papers, the January 6 attempt to overthrow the government—convinced me he would never be voted into any public office again. How wrong I was!

When Richard Nixon caused a constitutional crisis by firing attorney generals who were constitutionally charged with investigating his high crimes and misdemeanors, congressional representatives—Republicans—informed the President his malfeasance could not stand. Those Republicans put their country and their honor ahead of personal and party needs.

The Republicans of 2025 have put their cowardice and greed ahead of decency and duty to the nation. All of them save two have failed to honor the oath they swore to defend and protect the Constitution of the United States.

From the outset, January 21, 2025, there have been no elected or appointed insiders to keep the President from continuing his illegal and insane activities bent on destroying America. He surrounds himself with 'yes men and women' who are fundamentally determined to support his destructive policies and/or are cowed into submission by fear of losing their advantages of personal greed and lust for power. To date, there has been no effective opposition to this aberration of national leadership.

The Viet Nam war ended when the American public demonstrated it no longer supported the militaristic hawks who sought to prolong the war. An antiwar movement that materialized during the Johnson presidency was strong, growing and increasingly vocal. The American public listened, and for a multitude of reasons turned against the war. The Congress of that time took note and finally refused President Gerald Ford's request for continued war effort funding. That Congress put the will of the people ahead of a losing cause, and for America the war ended.

The current war is against 'We, the People.' It is against American values of fairness, decency, and rule of law. It is against the Constitution of the United States. This war is supported by DOGE, ICE, MAGA and the acquiescence and silence of nearly all Republicans. It is a war that can only be honorably ended by overwhelming opposition of patriotic American citizens, 'We, the People.'

A few days following Trump's inauguration, several alarmed persons began voicing their *opposition to his policies and activities. Modest demonstrations occurred. Although two Republicans, Adam Kinzinger and Liz Cheney, sacrificed their political careers rather than submit to Trump's infamy, the Republican Party lined up behind him ignoring the fact that he had tried to overthrow the government they had sworn to protect and preserve. The lesson was clear—speak up and you will be destroyed.*

In the beginning, hardly any Democrats voiced public disapproval, privately admitting their legislative impotence. As we stood by, the antics of Republican Trump, DOGE, ICE, and their MAGA supporters became sickening and shameful. While we waited for others to act for us, the 'co-presidency' of Musk and Trump charged ahead, destroying everything in their path. Finally, we began to understand that we had to act for ourselves.

A favorite niece of mine posted her opposition to MAGA/DOGE/ICE policies with the comment, "I cannot remain silent." It bothered me. I, an older uncle, had marched against the war in Viet Nam, campaigned on behalf of liberal democratic candidates, and claimed to be on the right side of history, but I had said nothing against this burgeoning threat to democracy and national well-being. "Do Something" Michele Obama said at the Democratic Convention. I decided the best I could do is voice my opposition to the madness of this Republican president. I, too, 'cannot remain silent.'

My dissent is in the pages that follow. Most of this material was submitted as Facebook Stories and Posts. A few entries are Comments on other people's Posts. *All are my words and my responsibility. I call my opposition Defiance.*

I Write Posts

I write posts not because Facebook readers need further enlightenment but to add my voice to those standing up against the ridiculousness of Republican Trumpism. MAGA/ DOGE/ ICE demonstrate on a daily basis their bankruptcy of morality and total incompetency. Trumpist inanities may be normal for acolyte Republican cult enablers but in the real world every word Trump utters is the product of an insane man. One day, hopefully soon, a reckoning will come.

It's not essential to me whether anyone reads my posts. These posts may or may not be important to readers depending upon whether they gain something worth their time spent. What is important to me is that I put words on a page, that I articulate my thoughts and ideas during these times of deceit, superficiality, and ignorance. I'm not a historian, but I believe the United States currently faces a crisis not equaled since the Civil War. It is a crisis of our own making, and it will metastasize into a national tragedy if we allow it. It may, but not with my acquiescence.

My upbringing took place in a politically liberal state, Minnesota. During my youth, my state's politicians followed a tradition of promoting liberal causes that benefited middle class working people who populated rural areas and small communities. Except for national elections that occurred every four years, all politics were local. The important issues were about school board meetings, a rural electrification project, county snow plowing, the independent telephone party line, and mail delivery.

The first time I ever heard a national political leader's name was when my father refused to accompany my mother to the polling place because she wanted to vote for Republican Dwight D. Eisenhower over Democrat Adlai Stevenson. The issue was resolved four years later when they both voted for John F. Kennedy.

While growing up on a small farm, working in the barns and fields under the 'tutelage' of my father, I heard a lot of words about the benefits of self-reliance, duty, and independence, but not from my father. Those 'flowery' words weren't his way of speaking. He said things like "Can't you figure it out yourself?" and "That's your job—nobody gets to sit around and do nothing," and "God damnit, do I have to tell you everything!" These were harsh words for my eight to sixteen year old ears, but they were said with love and the determination that he wasn't going to allow his son to become a do nothing freeloader. The worst sin one could commit, my father believed, was to be a parasite who didn't do his part. He despised Republicans.

The smartest kid in my high school class, Colin, got to go to Boy's State and participate in simulated government exercises, mock campaigns, and development of legislative proposals. Hubert Humphrey introduced Colin to John F. Kennedy during his fall campaign for President.

I was impressed, and more than a little envious. Several years later, after Kennedy had been killed, Johnson had abdicated and Nixon was in office, I was despairing to Colin how things had really gone to hell in a handbasket. He said something like, 'No,

Ivan, you got it wrong. Now is the time we prepare for better, not wallow in worse.' He went to work for the American Friends Service Committee, and I went into the Peace Corps. Thoughts of electoral politics became distant memories.

My hopes were revived with the candidacies of Robert F. Kennedy, Eugene McCarthy, George McGovern and later, Paul Wellstone. Even Hubert Humphrey, late to oppose the Viet Nam war, was nevertheless a better candidate than Richard Nixon. I worked in the California McGovern campaign; gave verbal support to Eugene McCarthy and voted for Hubert Humphrey. The American voting public disagreed; Nixon was elected, twice. 'Well, hell's bells,' I thought, 'enough wasting time.' I took up fly fishing, log house building, and got serious about pursuing an academic research career.

Several years elapsed. Bill Clinton was elected. He was a small town, rural kid like me. I could identify with that. His wife, Hillary, spoke adamantly and had an unflinching determination. I could admire that. Then Barak Obama came on the scene with a verbal eloquence that captured everyone's imagination. I volunteered myself to making telephone calls for the Obama campaign. We won!

But even the rescue of the American economy after Republicans forced the United States into a financial crisis with the collapse of the housing market ended with eight years of repressed Democratic governance stymied by Republican obstructionism. After the first two years, the Republican majority used their control of Congress to neutralize nearly every law that the democrats wished to enact. One, the *Affordable Care Act*, was enacted into law with the help of a single Republican vote, that of Senator John McCain. Following his support of health care for all, McCain was vilified by his Republican colleagues who attempted a hundred times to overturn the *Affordable Care Act*. Whether it will survive the Trump regime is uncertain.

A non-politician businessman, Donald J. Trump, followed Barak Obama into the White House. During his initial four years, this President managed to turn the American presidency into a joke. He earned the disrespect of leaders of other countries who barely concealed their snickers about him behind his back. His reputation as a failed businessman, recipient of six bankruptcies, court ordered payments to defrauded victims, lawsuits by unpaid contractors, convictions for sexual abuse incidents, and many other faults turned Donald J. Trump, President of the United States, into a national and international embarrassment.

Trump's denial of the efficacy of medical science and vaccines almost caused him to forfeit his life to the Covid 19 disease. For months during his first presidency, he had lived in a state of denial, hoping snake oil remedies and/or nature would reduce the Covid 19 pandemic's effects to the level of a common cold. When that didn't happen, he blamed the Chinese for creating the epidemic to attack the United States. Fortunately, against Trump's ignorance and rejection of scientific facts, world scientists were able to develop a vaccine and antiviral treatment that neutralized the deadly effects of the covid disease.

After Trump was voted out of office, the incoming democratic Biden administration treated Covid 19 like the threat to humanity it was. Under Biden's leadership, the government poured enormous American resources together with coordinating world-wide care directed at eradicating it. (Incidentally, the development of vaccines and unlimited distribution saved the lives of my wife and myself, who along with millions of other people around the world contracted the disease but were relieved of its worst effects by being vaccinated and taking the antiviral medication, Paxlovid.)

Unwilling to accept the results of the 2020 election which he lost, Trump incited a riot and attempted to prevent Congress from certifying the results on January 6, 2021. The insurrection failed, and the new government was installed against the wishes and votes of a majority of elected Republicans. Nevertheless, instead of being sent to prison in disgrace as he should have been, Democratic prosecutors weaseled and waffled away their dutiful opportunity while Make Government Great Again (MAGA) Republicans lied and cheated their way back into the White House.

At the end of President Biden's four years in office, Trump managed to avoid all of the legal problems he had created for himself. He convinced enough MAGA voters to reinstall him in the ultimate position of power, and this time chose only devoted 'yes men' worshippers and loyalists to rule with him. Unconvinced that his lies and obscene behaviors made him unfit for the office of President of the United States, Trump's voters sent him back to the White House for another four years.

In his first one hundred days, Donald J. Trump caused more havoc, pain, illegalities, and destruction than any other president in American history. He also caused a substantial portion of the American public to rise up against his policies and programs. The resistance to Trump rule, a defiance that grows every week, continues.

Peace Corps Inoculators

Among the earliest of Donald Trump's proposed cabinet members was Robert F. Kennedy, Jr. The son of one of America's most respected politicians, Kennedy's on again, off again opposition to several aspects of medical science including universal vaccinations earned him the disapproval of knowledgeable research scientists and medical doctors who cautioned his theories and recommendations were at best wrong and at worst lunacy.

This opposition did not derail his appointment prospects, especially in the light of Donald Trump's earlier recommendation that people inject antifreeze into their bodies to avoid dying from Covid 19. Even a close Kennedy cousin, Caroline Kennedy, the daughter of President John F. Kennedy, felt she could not remain silent and gave a public condemnation of the proposed appointment. Nevertheless, Kennedy Jr. was appointed to lead the nation's medical establishment as the Secretary of Health and Human Services.

Kennedy's appointment was opposed by Democrats, but they were unable to keep him from being confirmed by the Republican majorities in Congress. In that position, he holds sway over Centers for Disease Control and Prevention, and the National Institutes of Health. His first action was to fire 5,200 newly hired health workers. Prior to Kennedy, America prided itself on leading the world in the abolition of infectious diseases. A previous Republican president, George Bush, sponsored a seminal intervention against AIDS in Africa. This was continued by Trump's immediate predecessor,

12

Barak Obama. Upon assuming office for his second term, Trump pulled out of funding the project and withdrew the United States from the World Health Organization. HIV-AIDS deaths are expected to increase by 500,000 because of these actions.

In the summer of 1967, a group of Peace Corps Volunteer nurses arrived in country for service. Their assignment under the auspices of the World Health Organization was to eradicate smallpox from the world. This particular group was assigned to target remote provinces of Afghanistan.

Being mostly women--unrelated men, especially kafirs, or unbelievers were not allowed into Islamic households--these early twenty year old females traveled to inaccessible villages over Himalayan paths even a mountain goat would be challenged to negotiate.

Although vaccinated themselves, nevertheless these nurses risked their lives while identifying cases of smallpox and then vaccinating every person for miles around until there was no chance of further contagion. Their work together with other similarly assigned volunteers elsewhere in the world was a phenomenal success; for all practical purposes, smallpox no longer exists to afflict disease and death on world populations.

It is ironic that the current U.S. health secretary, a nephew of President John F. Kennedy, resists universal vaccination as a means of disease prevention, a posture that his own father, Attorney General Robert F. Kennedy, would never have countenanced. The Peace Corps still is President

Kennedy's most lasting legacy; what will be his nephew's claim to honor?

American Values

In the chaotic situation of world politics, especially the politics being promoted by the present political regime in the United States, any guiding sense of moral values has disappeared. Racism, sexism, misogyny, and dishonesty have become normal and acceptable. Half of our elected officials aggressively support a convicted felon who occupies the White House while the other half blindly acquiesces by wringing its hands in noisy silence. Hunger, starvation, genocide, and disease are allowed to afflict millions of people with barely a whisper from those who can and should help. We are no longer ashamed to watch children die under the bombs of tyrants, bombs that we ourselves manufacture and distribute worldwide.

Is there no morality left in America? Kant's categorical imperative—'Act only according to that maxim whereby you can at the same time will that it should become universal law'—i.e. 'what you are willing to apply to others you should be willing to apply equally to you', combined with the first principle of medical practice, 'do no harm', should be simple enough to understand and exercise by those who are elected to propose and enforce laws.

My introduction to the intellectual idea of values began when I took several philosophy courses in undergraduate college. Among the philosophers we studied were Socrates, Plato, and Aristotle. What impressed me was the message that philosophical ideas weren't restricted to the high brows of the major universities but could be discussed as drivers of real situations and influence the mental and physical behaviors of real people.

Not being a person interested in religious dogma, I tried to ignore the canon of the church, preferring instead to read decidedly unreligious writings of Sartre, Camus, Kafka and even Wittgenstein. Yet, one could not avoid Bishop Berkeley's ideas of God, Hume's skepticism, and Kant's moral imperative. The latter, Kant, impressed me most because of his requirement of fairness, that whatever laws are imposed they should be agreeable for and applicable to all people.

Bertrand Russell wrote an essay, 'Why I Am Not a Christian' in which he answered, 'because most Christians are not behaving as Christians' in their beliefs and actions. He also held the philosophical belief that those who make assertions should be able to back them up with rational proofs.

During these times of Republican control—those who know the price of everything and the value of nothing—funds for universities and colleges are being cut back, and anything that smacks of diversity, equity, and inclusion (DEI) is being banned. When funds are cut back, arts, music, theater, and philosophy programs are the first to suffer, and along with them creativity, imagination, and free thinking become an anathema. Values that are not in direct service of the ruling class— i.e. MAGA, DOGE, ICE, and their complaisant oligarchs—are tabu.

Pounce and Smell

I have a problem. I promised myself I wouldn't use the names of the two charlatans who have overtaken the government in my posts. Why should I, who despises everything they stand for, give them additional name recognition? But here's the problem—I need 'alternate facts' that will do the job just as well without being too vague or arrogant.

'Orange' doesn't work because it's mellow, and although 'drunk' is a play on sound, its intended target claims not to drink alcohol so it could be a lie. I don't want my behaviors to be aligned with theirs in any way. The self-anointed 'king's' namesake is used as a ploy to overpower face cards in bridge; maybe I can get by with an alternative word, 'pounce.' That's pretty close to the methods the terrible twins are using to force legions of federal workers out of their jobs right now.

The other one is not so difficult. In an earlier post, I referenced 'musk' as "a strong reddish-brown substance"--a dictionary definition I got off the internet. Being careful not to use a four-letter word, I've decided the word 'smell' will be an adequate descriptor that will work just as well for the richest man on earth.

So, for the time being, that's what it is, Pounce and Smell. I'm sure a lot of those workers who were just robbed of their jobs will see the irony in that. Do you? (If so, press Like; I'm sorry there is no indicator for MAGA people to use, but remaining silent is perfectly acceptable.)

Note: Later, I backed away from name calling. Donald Trump comes up with any number of ridiculous nicknames for people which he intends to be demeaning to them. I apologize for falling into the same verbal behavior, but I don't wish to mimic Trump in any way. Nevertheless, I've left these posts in their original form.

As this book is being edited, Elon Musk has left the government with the statement, "I can't take it anymore!" What he cannot take anymore was left ambiguous, but he did call the "big, beautiful bill" that the Republicans were passing through Congress "abominable." His exit from public life has illuminated much of the "take" that Musk has enjoyed through his association with President Trump.

Castles in the Sand: a moral tale

My posts are like castles in the sand. Some are elaborate, many turreted structures with crenellated walls and dungeons for culprits like Pounce and Smell (see previous Post). Others are crude outlines of square buildings waiting for incarceration of the miscreants who are currently destroying America. A few of my sand castles are small, barely noticeable on the beach cluttered with umbrellas and beer cans while others are massively adorned with tomes of roads and paths for an enterprising social reformer to follow.

But, like this one, all are merely castles in the sand, soon to be wiped out by the waves of Facebook's algorithmic censor that only allows one minute before extinction takes over. No matter, there are a lot of grains of sand to arrest the political trash left on the beach each night, polluting the first expanse of brightness where nature meets civilization in the never-ending struggle for an uncluttered sea of existence. I have no remorse; broken glass was once sand itself and with my help will become sand again.

Even while I was writing these Posts, the Facebook algorithm was being adjusted to limit the language and objects described. Word recognition, or certain character strings, are identified and used to raise 'flags' about their authors. Since my posts seemed to immediately 'age-out' I assumed I was being censored by Big Brother. Likely not in my case. In the scheme of things, my words are timid and unimportant), but in the light of DOGE and ICE, it is not absurd to assume Big Brother is watching. If you think this is preposterous, consider the government's installation of 'No Fly' and 'Watch' lists, and that 'face recognition' in Trump world means the color or tint of one's skin.

So Sad

My heart cries for those Federal workers who are losing their jobs because of the actions of Pounce and Smell, the (hopefully temporary) occupants of America's co-presidency.

I've been there. My supervisor invited me to a congenial 'coffee and caramel rolls' break one spring morning. My work was caught up, and I had no other appointments. After small talk reminiscing about my infant daughter and newly mortgaged house occasioned by my recent resettlement into the job I then held, that supervisor said with a somber look of total commiseration, "I'm sorry, Ivan, but there is no place in the budget for you anymore."

I tried to maintain a professional composure, but I was stunned. I was being let go, fired if you will, because of a Republican governor's 'recission' of the funds my employer had used to support my position. (Fortunately, I survived because of my union's successful lawsuit against the Republican governor's recission action.)

These federal workers, targets of Pounce and Smell, are not freeloaders doing bad jobs for America. I appreciate that my local Social Security agent helped me negotiate the jungle of regulations I faced when it came time for me to retire. I thank the medical researchers who discovered heart drugs that keep me healthy during these later years. I know if I hadn't been vaccinated I would have died from Covid 19. And I'm happy that those federal employees, without exception, did their best to keep America functioning as a democracy.

The dictatorship being pursued by Pounce and Smell and all of their Republican acolytes must be defeated. "Have you no sense of decency?" was asked of Republican Senator Joseph McCarthy who had also embarked years ago in a self-aggrandizing attack on American workers. McCarthy faded into an inglorious history, but his shame has permeated the Republican ruling class again. Stop it! Now!

Particularly egregious was the fact that the people who were forcing federal workers out of their jobs were faceless, largely incompetent, and ignorant of the value of the work that the people they were firing were doing. Later, after protests and belated recognition, many were hired back.

How could they ever forget the insult, the trauma, and the humiliation foisted upon them by the DOGE operatives? Even with the exit of Elon Musk from his self-aggrandized position of authority, the damage DOGE has done lives on and continues to destroy America.

Morning Coffee

I ask myself, 'what have my two North Dakota Republican Senators done to assist citizens of the Peace Garden State lately?' Let me count the ways...

*Passing a law that will help a few North Dakota billionaires increase their wealth (they don't live here but extract their money from the ND economy).

*Cheering Smell (my nickname for him) as he wrecks the American government by sending federal workers to the unemployment lines (that is, lines of unemployed people sans benefits).

*Taking away the one really good TV channel, PBS, by fostering cuts to their funding (trashing Prairie Public was done by the Republican state legislature, but extinction at the federal level is underway).

*Journeying to Florida to kiss the ring of the new King (self-proclaimed, not from a royal family) and genuflect to the unelected co-president.

*Installing their billionaire friends in Pounce's (my nickname for him) cabinet and other positions that control the most sensitive agencies of our government—State, Military, Homeland Security, Energy, Environment, Social Security, etc.

*Driving up the price of coffee, eggs, and most groceries lately.

*Doubling measles in Texas and New Mexico in one week, nearly all cases verified to be among unvaccinated children.

*Ignoring a new strain of covid (unverified warning from a Chinese lab in Wuhan). Over a million Americans and seven million people worldwide died from Covid 19.

In short, North Dakota's two senators are partisans enabling the destruction of what was the most successful democracy in the history of the world (although Plato's Greece did admirably well). From my perspective, the one positive thing these two senators have done with their support of Pounce and Smell is enrage sleeping democrats and one or two ostrich Republicans to 'throw the bas***ds out!' It can't happen too quickly.

"...'tis a consummation Devoutly to be wish'd..." said Hamlet. Even as this is being written, Republicans are losing their hold on local and state positions, bringing rational human beings hope that there will be a decisive change in the political environment after the next fall elections.

The 'sleeping democrats' were biding their time to let the Republicans 'hang themselves.' Unfortunately, the American public was left hanging with them, and it wasn't until significant numbers of protestors took to the streets that Democrats began to act. Better late than never.

Hamlet's Revenge

"The play's the thing wherein we'll catch the conscience of a king..."

Waiting for Lefty, a 1935 play by Clifford Odets, involves discussions among workers oppressed by the rule of corrupt union bosses and greedy owners of production. They wait for Lefty to tell them what to do. By inaction, people forfeit the ability to resist. Lefty never comes; he was shot on the way to the meeting.

These are apprehensive times. The remaining question is, will an as yet unacknowledged person with a voice of reason and decency rise to the occasion, or will enraged armed lunatics like those of January 6 be allowed to destroy American democracy?

Congressional Democrats and closeted disgruntled Republicans embrace their impotence by hiding behind minority statuses and electoral complacency while screaming uprightly to their constituents. We are having none of it. In the Bard's words, all of their sound and fury signifies nothing. A popular awakening has occurred in every state of the Union and the elected leadership sits on its hands, waiting...

I would add, 'waiting' while public outrage is growing, a welcomed change but fraught with danger. There are a lot of crazy people carrying guns who in their enraged delirium feel they have the right to hurt people they don't like. 'Beware of the devil you seek for you may be that devil.'

Bounce Back Alive

I propose Congress pass a law (BBA) to ameliorate the damage caused by the damning duo and their billionaire Republican acolytes in the White House. This law will provide five years of full salary funding for every person who has been fired by Pounce and Smell. A quotation from Shakespeare, *'The evil that men do lives after them...'* is my justification for suggesting five years of funding for BBA. Recipients only need to show their RIF email or text messages to qualify.

The funding for this law should come from an amendment naming the 'Pounce' Cabinet members, complicit congress members, and other billionaire hangers-on like Bezos, Zuckerberg, Koch, the Murdochs and several Waltons as compulsory contributors of ten million dollars or more each per year (Putin also qualifies as an 'influencer' member of Pounce's Cabinet and should do his part after he pays for the suffering and damage he has forced on Ukraine). Smell should be required to provide a full dollar match as he is the prime mover in this catastrophe. Until TESLA goes bankrupt, he can afford it.

American democracy, if it survives the current administration, will need recovery time. One year after the Pounce regime retires is a minimum. The quotation continues with *'the good is oft interred with their bones.'* We'll trust the timing of their demise up to the gods, the final arbiters in all things human. I don't wish to aggrandize the terrible co-presidents or trivialize the issue by labeling their deeds human, but I do think the perpetrators should absorb the shame and feel the pain of the world they will have wrought.

My law provides an opportunity for some good to emanate from the Pounce and Smell ravages.

Note: I wrote "Until TESLA goes bankrupt…." This appears to be more than a fanciful possibility. TESLA lost more than 50% of its stock value while Mr. Musk was playing at destroying the government.

Ne Nothi Te Deorsum

Where this day's madness began is debatable. Maybe it was with Barry Goldwater's statement, *"I would remind you that extremism in the defense of liberty is no vice! And let me remind you also that moderation in the pursuit of justice is no virtue!"*

That is, Pounce and Smell will try any method they can to destroy America, and the Democratic response will be weak and ineffectual. Take notice: it isn't liberty the Republican cult is after, it is freedom to exercise unbridled authoritarianism. Justice and the rule of law reined in Goldwater's America, but that system of public values is being extinguished by the current Republican MAGA cadre of law breakers.

Americans are awakening in every State of the Union. Protests, lawsuits, boycotts, signs, editorials, town halls, arrests, resistors, petitions, and rightfully directed anger are causing the privileged elected class to take notice. Suddenly, those guaranteed lucrative salaries for elected legislators are not so certain. The plushy offices and lunch pavilions are not as inviolable. Limousines and first class airplane tickets are not as comfortable.

Ne Nothi Te Deorsum is pidgin Latin for Don't Let the Bastards Get You Down. I first heard the phrase over thirty years ago in Kentucky at a convention of people with disabilities who were seeking legislation to alleviate social and physical barriers to get through doorways, into busses, up staircases, through serving lines, etc. These folks weren't disabled people; they were people with disabilities; they aren't handicapped; they are people with handicaps. They fight and they endure, and they win their battles. They are still fighting. We will too.

This King has No Conscience

Whereas Clifford Odet's Lefty was a wished-for hero who didn't arrive (he was shot), Samuel Beckett's anti-hero in *Waiting for Godot* (1953) doesn't show up because he never existed in the first place. Waiting for something that never was demonstrates the absurdity of striving for an existence than can never be.

Waiting for Trump to act like a rational man is equally absurd and thinking any possible good can come out of Pounce, Retreat* and Smell is dumb. Yesterday's Oval Office performance revealed the absolute inanity of electing two infantile schoolyard bullies. Any two ten year olds who acted like they did with President Zelenskyy would have been told to stand in a corner until they could get a slap down from their parents.

These three people—Pounce, Retreat and Smell--have shamed us all not only in the United States but throughout the world. They are dragging us through the putrid slime of their existence, releasing a stench that even the worst despots (excepting the genocidists Putin, Netanyahu, and their enablers) are reluctant to abide. The shame, the shame.

Retreat is my nickname for Vance. Technically, Putin is a war criminal for dropping bombs on children because he has a declared war with Ukraine, whereas Netanyahu's killing of thousands of kids rises to the level of genocide because he claims his war is with Hamas, not Palestine.

Convicted felon Trump is a piker because his crimes are menial by comparison.

Rivers of My Mind

In perusing my four novels, I see that I've spent a lot of sentences talking about rivers—the Mississippi, Schoolcraft, Kabul River, Buffalo (Bison) river, Missouri river, and the Red River of the North. I like rivers. They were the American highways of earlier centuries and still are time passages for young kids.

As a pre-teenager, my friend and I spent hours and days rowing up the Mississippi and Schoolcraft rivers from Carr Lake, staring into the water in search of turtles and fish.

On the inside bend of a meandering stream the current hollows out deep holes, the homes of river walleyes. Northern pike inhabit the shallower parts of the river beds hiding in the water grasses in the early summer. In places where trees overhang the water, rock bass rest in the shade. Cattails and lily pads conceal black bass. Big northerns spawn in the spring while ice is still solid on the river banks. Walleyes swim in the middle of the stream when their spawning is over, and suckers and Red Horse travel up the river to spawn in the muddy flats, rushing in front of our boat numbering in the hundreds.

When I had gotten over the thrills of catching any kind of fish of any size, my interests turned to ocean fishing for salmon. The two largest fish I ever caught were King Salmon from the ocean on a charter out of Ilwaco. Even so, I never forgot the river. Around each bend is a new experience—a mother duck and a whole covey of little ones, a pair of loud geese, a muskrat or beaver swimming to the bank, eagles sitting on a bare branch, a swarm of river hatch bugs, fallen trees, rapids, sometimes a blue heron. The river is a continuous stream of discovery, especially for a young mind.

I don't spend much time on the river any more. Now I write of rivers from my memory. In *Murder at Coffee Pot Landing* I wrote of a wide spot behind a Mississippi river beaver dam. My Kabul River experiences in Afghanistan were told in *The Phantom Djinn*. The Red River of the North appears in *The River Walk Child* as does the same river with a fictionalized presence in *Bison River Madam*. Rivers are a metaphor for life. 'Old man river, he just keeps rolling along.'

River and stream pollution is ranked among America's greatest environmental disasters and represents one of its most pressing needs. Retraction of funds for amelioration has to be recognized as a callousness that even surpasses usual Republican backwardness. Not content with wrecking the government, DOGE is killing the environment as well.

We Gather, We Sing, We Protest

We gather, we sing, we protest. In some venues its warming to spring, other places still hold the freezing cold of winter. Some of us wear heavy coats while others dress in summer clothes. We gather, we sing, we protest. Each day, each weekend, our crowds grow larger. Our rhetoric is no longer subdued; now speakers call for aggressive accountability, for justice and if it does not come, for a more certain resolution. Jail for the perpetrators, a rail for the hangers-on.

Hiding in their offices, cancelling long-scheduled community meetings, faking urgent phone calls from absent callers, elected Republican MAGA officials pretend importance where only their shame and cowardice reveals their deceit. We gather, we sing, we protest.

What laws are we breaking? Are there laws against decency, familial sanctity, protection of one's livelihood? Is due process really just fifteen minutes for vacating one's profession, cancelling one's financial security, destroying one's present and future happiness, placing one in lengthening unemployment lines? We gather, we sing, we protest.

Prufrock asks, "Have I the strength to force the moment to its crisis?" More of us are answering that question, and when the tide turns, MAGA won't like the wash. We gather, we sing, we protest. And, in two years, we vote!

As the cold winter turned to spring, protestors began to march on sidewalks, bridges, in front of offices and government buildings, and at Republican and Democratic events. Their persistence and dedication has led to protests taking place in every state, city, and country location in the United States. As this is being written, a national uprising is planned for June 14, 2025, as a counter protest to Trump's military parade.

Cheating Time

Well, Pounce, you can cheat on your lenders and cheat on your investors, you can cheat on your voters and cheat on your wives, you can cheat on your buddies and cheat on your friends, you can cheat on your golf scores and cheat on your taxes, but, Pounce, there is one thing even you can't cheat on. You can't cheat on the ringing bells of time.

Time is a great democratizer; it brings down mighty trees and short grasses. Time spares no friends and spares no enemies. Rich or poor, young or old, time does one thing consistently well, Pounce. It passes. Your time will recede like the echoes of an old church bell, bouncing around the dark smelly alleys of your life.

Here's how. It begins with a tinkle in the back of your mind, an advisor whispering you should never do that. You proceed, and in a short time, that tinkle becomes a discordance in both of your ears. Democrats on one side compete with retired Republicans on the other to chastise you for your intemperance. Next, there is the roar of your January 6 and MAGA friends banging on empty barrels telling you to leave their kids, parents, and jobs alone. Now Mexicans, Chinese and Canadians join in with their tariff sabers beating against the cannons of your trade wars.

You are no longer in control of your own madness; your insanity has taken on a life of its own. 'Never send to know for whom the bell tolls; it tolls for thee.' –said John Donne. Bells are ringing for you, Pounce, do you hear them?

Crime and Punishment

Your crimes, Pounce, haven't risen to the genocidal levels of Stalin, Hitler, and Genghis Khan (yet) but given the company you keep you may soon be able to take your place among the worst of the worst. Already, together with your predecessor in the Oval Office, you are complicit in war crimes by providing lip service to Putin's atrocities and sending more bombs for Netanyahu to explode.

Is not the total ruination of two countries enough? Does the last child walking in the Gaza rubble have to be killed? Do you relish seeing a Ukrainian baby's dead hand reach out from under the burning planks of a destroyed Kiev home? When will the last soldier die? Whose son or daughter will that conscript be?

You may get away with it, Pounce. You'll not be led into court again to account for your crimes. Convictions on thirty-four counts will be enough. Your fate will not be like Mussolini's to be strung up feet first with your head pointing to the hell you deserve. Nuremberg will not host your final courtroom appearance before incarceration. You may have aged out of molesting female reporters, grabbing starlets, and storing classified materials in your bathroom so additional felony charges may be few.

No need to worry Pounce—if you are successful in selling the FBI buildings, exposing CIA operatives around the world, and dispensing with the Secret Service (be careful with that one--they are the only thing saving you from martyrdom and you shouldn't count on Proud Boys and other January 6 residue; they're busy terrorizing southern border immigrants!) By defunding the police and firing the lawyers, there will be no one to arrest you for any new crimes. Finally, unless you disband them, you will always have your Supreme Court to backstop any future activities from becoming actionable crimes.

I am reminded of a rhyme written by Oscar Wilde:

We know not whether laws be right
Or whether laws be wrong.
All we know who lie in gaol
Is that [prison] walls are strong...

And that's where you belong, Pounce, that's where you belong.

Take note, Donald, one of your Supreme Court judges is demonstrating a propensity to put legal integrity over loyalty to you. This judge is not turning against you; rather, the judge is upholding the laws of the country that they, too, swore to defend.

Golden Rule

"Do unto others as you would have them do unto you," is essentially a statement of selfishness. It presumes others would like you to 'do unto' them; it presumes what you would 'do unto' them is something you and they would both want; it presumes they would choose to act on 'do unto you.' And so on. This is not a golden rule, it's a rule of gold. Let me explain.

Pounce and Smell have embarked on a mission of 'destroy, destroy, destroy—fire, fire, fire.' That which is being reduced to ashes are not the empires they built for themselves. It is your homes, professions, finances, families, educations, health, and futures that you built for your families that are being consumed in the fires of their hell on earth. Out of your ashes they are constructing bigger fortunes for themselves. Like Goldfinger, they are men with the Midas touch.

Unlucky MAGA voters are finding the co-presidents to be non-discriminatory 'trashers.' MAGA's who voted for Pounce are finding they are also being given their fifteen minutes to clear out their offices.

'Whoops, don't take the staplers; they belong to us now.'

When MAGA voters cry out, they're told, 'but that's what you voted for—it's what we said we'd do!'

'But I meant them,' MAGAs complain, 'not me! You are supposed to vanquish the terrible DEI and WOKE democrats. I didn't mean for you to fire me.'

Those MAGA voters, the same ones who brought Pounce and Smell into our lives, do not repent. They don't recognize the error of their actions. In their minds they haven't done anything to deserve the treatment they're getting. They don't find any folly in their vote. Their intent was to impact the lives of others, not their own. Their golden rule is, 'screw you; I'm getting mine now.' Shame on you, MAGA, shame on you.

I vaguely remember a story from the church days of my youth about this guy who angrily tipped over the moneylenders' tables that were obstructing an entrance to the temple. Could it happen again?

Painful Observations

It was painful and sad to see the Presidency of the United States so degraded. The pain was not the viewer's alone. There were no highlights, but these are my observations.

She descended the balcony steps, the Queen of Pounce, Himself the would-be King. In her best nightclub attire, she moved with the studied gait of a runway diva from yesteryear, unsure if her stilettoed heels were up to the job of supporting her middle-aged weight. Her face, not totally insincere, evidenced pain as if she had just been verbally mauled in a domestic dispute. During the evening she revealed a faraway defeated and sadly blank look.

Sitting next to her was a very pale faced red lipped young woman, making the contrast with the Queen all the more stark. One thing is sure, the not-so-divine Miss M should fire the cosmetics advisor who cast her face in the orange tones of her husband's hair. Last evening was not a win for her.

The Justices marched in, nodding to their appreciative acolytes as they made their way to front row seats. Their faces were stoic, without emotion or human recognition of any kind as they settled into their chairs with practiced ambivalence. Even the most recently ensconced of them, a handsome, once youthful woman plucked from oblivion by her Lord, portrayed the high court's aura of apathy and indifference.

If only one could read their minds, would they be thinking about how this impostor, this co-king whom they made unaccountable for past, present, and future crimes, was destroying the very Constitution they swore to uphold? Is there any among them who entertain forbidden thoughts of remorse and repeal? What will they decide when the next anointment trial comes their way?

Perhaps the most pathetic of all present were the men and women seated on both sides of the aisle. To Pounce's left were Republican Congress people, jumping-jack cult admirers of their Master's pronouncements. Their signalers, the two men who presided over the convocation, bounced up and down with glee at every profound word, showing the adoring crowd it was also time for them to genuflect.

The vassal seated the right, the reigning vice president, showed hesitancy with all the animated bouncing, his fatigue unseen by the Godfather in front of him. He glanced enviously at the billionaire Cabinet members who with satisfaction and loyal confidence know the fix is in. The others of the Congress, elected Democrats, sat glumly by in resignation and defeat. A few waved pathetic little oval signs with writing on them, others wore the pink costumes from eight years ago, and one—only one!—was ushered out by the chamber marshal for disturbing the peace and solemnity of the occasion. (I've seen dead people with more life than these representatives of the people showed.)

Grandest of all was the entrance of the co-Presidents. Surrounded by armies of January 6 and MAGA congressmen posing as ushers, they walked with magnificence, offering their rings to be kissed by some while abhorring the touch of many.

Again, it was Republican cult faces that were most striking. Each visage was imbued with eighty percent television smile and twenty percent fear. Were they afraid that they wouldn't be noticed by their Excellencies, or were they afraid that they would? 'Did I bow deeply enough? Was my red tie too ambitious?' They had learned from harsh experience that when the whale from Moby Dick set his eye on you, your ship was doomed.

"What about the speech?" you may ask. Oh, I'm sorry. There was nothing there—just whining, blaming, and lying. Forget it; it was empty of any meaningful content.

The aforementioned was written after watching President Trump's 2025 speech to Congress.

Profit is Theft!

"Profit is Theft" is a nostalgic phrase borrowed from Karl Marx in the 1960s by freaks bent on enraging the Establishment. Essentially, it encapsulated a simple question: when labor produces more value than the cost of production, who has the right to benefit from that excess, the laborer who did the work or the owner of the locale where the work was performed? Unions answered 'labor,' capitalists said 'owners.' Beatniks, hippies, yippies, and freaks all around the world said, 'Screw you, I'll do it my way.' Frank Sinatra and the mafia turned that phrase into a labor-busting anthem.

It's different now. Instead of surplus value we now struggle over surplus labor. The means of production are no longer workers. Real work is done by robots, computers, artificial intelligence, chemical fertilizers, miracle drugs, and for the rich, space ships, drones, laser-guided bombs, and compliant Republican dupes. The modern owners of high capacity production employ trophy wives, literati, charitable causes, endless made-for-tv awards to themselves, green-desert golf courses, and cloned broods of children to remind the less accomplished among us that we should revere how wonderful they are.

Profit is no longer theft; how does one steal from a machine? Profit for the Establishment is keeping what they are already taking from others. Walled communities (razor wire preferred for aesthetic effect), unimpregnable cars, a few railroads, big jet-powered aircraft, numbered offshore accounts, unbreakable passwords, massive land investments, skyscraper hotels, and most importantly, an admiring cult of Republican-assisted January 6 and MAGA devotees enable the thieves of the 21st century to have their licentious ways with us.

The titans of modern industry still control the means of production, but production is accomplished through computer algorithms, big box retail chains, transportation systems, lucrative government contracts, and political parties. The *End of Work* said Jeremy Rifkin in a 1995 book is upon us.

Multiple wives, child sex slaves, clandestine island retreats, Florida mansions, and jaunts to the Riviera are not enough to quench the greed of this new Establishment. They want our jobs, our kids, our education, our health, our environment, our social security, and the food from our tables.

In return, they say *"Let them eat cake!"* That didn't turn out so well for Marie Antoinette. We'll see how the New Establishment royalty does with it. Take note, New Establishment—uprisings are occurring in every state, city, and precinct of America. Your time may be nearly over.

Coincidence?

I'm puzzled, Pounce, downright bewildered. Undoubtedly, my bafflement comes from watching too many crime stories on television. In every one of them I hear a hardnosed prosecutor utter the phrases, "Detective, that's too coincidental for me to believe. Get out there, look again and come back with real evidence!" Sigh; more footwork for the men in blue who walk the streets knocking on doors to verify what everyone has been told is the unblemished obvious truth, 'There was no VOTER FRAUD!'

We heard on November 5, 2024, that you and Bouncy (my nickname based on his up and down performance during your recent report to Congress) won the Presidency fair and square by defeating your opponent in each of the seven tossup states. 'Fair and square,' that's what you said. But here's the rub, Pounce. My skeptical hardnosed prosecutor wants real proof, and s/he doesn't believe in coincidences. And, I would add, neither do you.

You said, over and over again during the campaign, that there had to be VOTER FRAUD in each of those seven states. Even more astounding, I now believe there was VOTER FRAUD in each of those seven states. The statistical 'law of unnatural coincidences' argues that the odds for a total electoral sweep were almost impossible. There had to be VOTER FRAUD. You even said so. Many times.

VOTER FRAUD being highly believable, we must ask, 'Whose VOTER FRAUD was it?' Common sense argues not the Democrats because it isn't credible for them to conduct VOTER FRAUD and then not win at least one or two tossup states. I know you say the Democrats are incompetent, but please, Pounce, use your head, they're not that bad! Democrat VOTER FRAUD doesn't even pass the Smell test.

Think about it; VOTER FRAUD in seven states would take a lot of money to pull off, especially if that VOTER FRAUD were to remain undiscovered. Democratic contributors don't have that kind of money. I mean jeeze, you'd have to be the richest man in the world to do something like that. Opps, I take that back. I don't want to accuse anyone of lying and cheating, corruption, and conspiracy without overwhelming and convincing evidence.

So here's the nub of it, Pounce. We have to impanel a Congressional Enquiry to look into the presence of VOTER FRAUD in each of those seven states. I propose the panel consist of legislators from non-tossup blue and red states. Their staffs could be recently unemployed DOJ lawyers, prosecutors and vote counters who suddenly have lots of time on their hands. I'm sure in the interests of fiscal austerity they will come cheaply. It's in your best interests, Pounce. You wouldn't want to be impeached for a third time based on flimsy, hearsay evidence, would you?

I Am Shocked

I'm shocked how quickly the MAGA triumvirate was allowed to dismantle and destroy the foundations of my American democracy. Naïve me, I believed my elementary grade school teachers who taught me that America was built on ideas of decency, equality, and fairness. 'Life, liberty, and the pursuit of happiness' were the basis of our fifth-grade civics classes. Biased as it was benefitting the ruling white class, the American dream was something I learned we should all buy into.

I grew up in a small, mid-western town where most people I knew were honest and fair-minded. They spoke well of one another and disdained those who did not. They shared their food, labor and even their homes when necessary. In the 1950s, my father let a homeless stranger sleep on our couch for a night in the middle of the winter. The man stayed three months; it seemed natural to us. When one of my siblings complained, my father said, 'What should I do, put him out in the freezing snow!' That was the end of that discussion, and we got used to occasional strangers sleeping on our couch.

It's time for a newly energized democratic party. We've lived off FDR's ideas for a hundred years, but now it's time to foster some new ideas, new programs, new processes and above all involve new people. We older people (I'm 84) have had our day; new faces are needed. A note of caution: don't prematurely shunt us out of the picture. We can still work to stymie the 'destruction regime' of Pounce, Bounce and Smell. That should be our main job.

Your job is to create a better world to come and not be tied to now outdated and backward thinking.

New people with fresh ideas, young and old, need to take charge. What to do? First, start dreaming about what should be. 'Should be' is a moral and political challenge. Base your new democratic thoughts on the philosophy of 'greatest good for the greatest number.' Find ways to take pride in the real meaning of America. Combine that with 'do no harm,' and we'll have a successful working agenda.

Articulate your dreams and thoughts. Get away from oligarchic platforms* (Facebook and the like) that thrive on pretty pictures, cheap shots, and clever snippets. Find a forum where the quality of your mind can be exhibited and implemented. A vibrant democracy needs evolution to bury the relics of the past. Meet, discuss, consider, and evaluate your ideas. Build a new democracy at every level by electing yourselves, not us (and certainly not MAGA), to positions of decision making and execution.

Finally, do it now. Don't wait for four years or two years or even 100 days to pass. Waiting breeds lethargy that prevents action. Let others sleep. It's your life, not theirs, that you are living. Enrich its possibilities by creating a new democratic nation.

Note: I apologize for my verbal arrogance. I am ashamed to admit that the destructive triumvirate exists because we allowed it to. MAGA told us what they would do if elected, and we chose to believe no one could be so evil and stupid. How wrong we were!

Since writing this Post, several national media commentators, influencers, politicians, and public figures have touted moving from Twitter, Face Book, and the like to an open, free, and uncensored platform called Blue Sky.

No Intelligent Life Here, Scotty

A joke from the past featured Captain Kirk's request, "Beam me up, Scotty, there's no intelligent life here," with a picture of Earth in the background.

I'm sympathetic to this view each time I consider the antics of Pounce, Bounce and Smell. Committing the United States to a national 'cryptocurrency' reserve may not be the most hurtful or damaging conspiracy the terrible duo has engaged in, but it is the dumbest (Bounce isn't counted; he has to ride in a trailer plane to mitigate the impact should God intervene.)

On the other hand, it may be a move in Pounce's genius economics. If he puts the whole $36 trillion national debt in the crypto pot together with the retirement money his obedient MAGA devotees will invest, both can disappear overnight into cyberspace with no one the wiser.

Had the Supreme Court not pre-emptively excused this dishonest leader of the free world from accounting for his stupidity, this idiotic venture into robbing the American public would have surely put him and his complicit relatives in ankle bracelets for the rest of their felonious lives. We can only hope, especially if gags accompany the sentencing of all three MAGA villains, that someday good sense will again prevail.

Note: The movement toward public investment in crypto currencies is growing regardless that several highly experienced and intelligent economists have labeled crypto as a scam, a Ponzi scheme, a fraud *and exceptionally risky. The Trump family is highly active in the crypto world, bragging that they maintain an immense posture in their version of the [fake] currency they've created.*

White Swans

White swans are said to symbolize love, loyalty, unity, and purity. Driving through the Minnesota lake country, pairs of swans can be seen resting on the ice of most ponds, lakes and at the edges of streams, waiting for the thaw that allows them to build nests. They are also said to bring wisdom, balance and grace to the country that hosts them.

Isn't it sad that ICE continues to arrest and deport desperate immigrants who come seeking white swan civilities that once characterized our America. Under the current regime, they are more likely to find black swans which in some European mythology heralded the work of the devil and promised a witches brew. (I don't wish to totally demean black swans; Oriental myths portray black swans having a much more beneficent nature.)

The conniving triptych continue their demolition of the American national character along with destruction of world economies and institutions of government. MAGA cheers them on while secretly praying the destruction will not reach them.

A few lines from William Butler Yeats say it well:

Things fall apart; the center cannot hold;

Mere anarchy is loosed upon the world,

The blood-dimmed tide is loosed, and everywhere

The ceremony of innocence is drowned;

The best lack all conviction, while the worst

Are full of passionate intensity.

Yeats saw the destruction from the First World War and witnessed the rise of Hitler and the Nazis who brought on an even worse Second World War. Is a new triumvirate of political oligarchs about to decimate the 21st century? It won't be long before we all know, and by then it may be too late.

Looming Financial Disaster

Like most retired people, I worry about my Social Security check disappearing from DOGE's panoply of dirty tricks. With it goes my health and auto insurance, property tax payments, monthly food allocation, hearing, eye and dental care, heart maintenance drugs, etc. I've earned money since I was fourteen and paid into the Social Security trust fund since I was eighteen—I got my Social Security card about the same time I registered for a draft card.

Direst of all, I will no longer afford the $9 haircuts I get at the local barber college and either revert back to hippiedom or become exposed to my wife's voracious scissors. If worse came to worse, I could become a 'greeter' at one of the big box stores, but with their cutbacks in employment and burgeoning bankruptcies those prospects are becoming slim to nothing also. Old people jobs are not plentiful anymore.

Many individuals are much worse off than people like me. Consider what happened to the economy this past week or so. It lost over a trillion dollars! Now, taking into account that over 50% of that 'lost wealth' was owned by the top 2% of people in the United States (including offshore tax avoiders), those poor folks lost so much money that my meager SS check wouldn't even make a showing in fifteen decimal rounding error (.000,000,000,000,001). What's a few dollars when they lost over half a trillion dollars? For example, the richest billionaire in the world may have to go back to digging for diamonds in South Africa, and the co-president may be forced to buy cheaper golf balls from K-Mart. 'Don't cry for me, Argentina.'

Back to Social Security. What could I expect being so foolish to trust in an 85 year old Ponzi scheme? Shame on me.

Note: My facetiousness may have overcome my better judgment when writing this Post. Social Security, Medicare, and Medicaid are serious issues not only for people my age but for millions of other people. Please read these words with your funny bone intact.

MAGA-TESLA

The co-president appears to have purchased a TESLA from his not quite as rich anymore buddy. Although many commentators quickly labeled this acquisition rank cronyism, it may instead be an example of MAGA presidential genius right out of *The Art of the Deal*.

If the pretty red car or ever-so-gruesome looking truck was purchased with government money, it technically belongs to the United States of America and therefore should be tax free. Assuming the vehicle was manufactured in the United States—not in, for example, in Canada, Mexico, China or even South Africa—it will not have import taxes levied against its purchaser. (Please, my god! do not call them tariffs! The Wall Street economists would freak out when they hear that word, and the stock market could lose another two trillion dollars.)

The vehicle was parked on the White House lawn. It probably qualifies as a 'used car' alleviating its owner from paying any new vehicle excise taxes. A side benefit for the two co-presidents is they can borrow a Fox News recording of their awe-inspiring sales performances to use as vita entries when they apply for used car salesmen positions at the burned out soon-to-be rebuilt Tesla dealerships in Washington, D.C. and New York. They'll need to work quickly to beat the TESLA bankruptcy filings soon to appear in complaisant courts.

An astute MAGA militarist would enjoy enormous foresight in a TESLA Truck purchase. Imagine, if you will, two automated machine guns mounted on the front fenders, controlled from the inside of the now camouflaged 'Tesla space crafted' mini tank. With satellite-guaranteed precision, guns could be maneuvered via Starlink, solely under the control of the DOGE mafioso's.

Take note, this technology is a little too complicated for the current Secretary of Defense to master; he needs to stick to combing his hair. As government surplus, not waste, fraud and abuse, the unused refitted tanks will certainly become a 'hit' with freed January 6 warriors. Maybe the vehicles will be collector's items in the 22 century.

Words Matter

Words matter. Who can forget the rallying cry of *'Liberte, Egalite, Fraternite'* of the French revolution, or the evil intent accompanying the words 'Heil Hitler.' *"Give me freedom or give me death!"* Nathan Hale said. *"A day that will live in infamy,"* was spoken by FDR at the outset of the Second World War. Merely whispering *'Black power'* sent shivers through racists everywhere, as does the more recent, *"Black Lives Matter."* Words and their elevation or suppression can take on a symbolic meaning far beyond what is common usage.

The Free Speech Movement (FSM) began in 1964 in Berkeley when Mario Savio jumped on a soap box and uttered a four letter 'f' word. The Establishment reacted with horror which guaranteed the verbal gesture a worldwide audience. Use of the 'f' word has become so common one is no longer shocked to hear it said in church, on the street, by teenagers, quoted by television anchors, and even on the floor of Congress. It appears on t-shirts, wrist bands, hats, and billboards. Half of the dialogue in Netflix and Amazon Prime include the WORD.

So you will not be surprised when I say that a new word, this one with five letters, has become the rallying cry of the 21st century. It's use is meant to be as revolutionary as was the 'f' word, but its meaning is abhorred by its users rather than its targets. It began as the name of a brilliant engineer, renowned for his far reaching achievements. After nearly drifting into obscurity, it was appropriated by a South African car salesman who elevated it as an advertising gimmick capable of moving economies and stock markets throughout the world. Its new owner became the richest man on earth.

What goes up must come down. TESLA stock has lost nearly 50% of its value in a few weeks, erasing $800 billion in market value. TESLA car sales have plummeted. TESLA dealerships are closing to avoid protesting crowds at their doors every day. In a few cases, TESLA vehicles have been vandalized, lit on fire, keyed, and splattered with paint and eggs. Owners hide their five-character symbols of affluence in garages, hoping to escape the anger of the multitudes striking back against the Empire. Owning a TESLA, once the darling of the 'in environmental class,' is now identified as the logo of an out-of-control marauding, predatory pair of capitalists.

Words matter.*

*Since writing this Post, a new word, TACO, referred to as Trump Always Chickens Out, has made its way into our lexicon.

Town Hall Blues

The MAGA Republicans hide from constituent Town Halls while righteous Democrats shadow box from the safe corners of their political domains. Social Security, federal jobs, health, education, and the First Amendment rights are daily fodder for 'rope-a-dope' politics. Both parties claim to foster truth, 'and would you please send us just 63 cents a day, or 19 dollars a month' is the modern statement of America's safety net.

Pictures of starving kids in Africa or brutalized animals in Schenectady are meant to tug our heart strings while loosening our wallets, rendering no need for government interventions. Even the Greatest President For All Time gets into the act by selling trinkets, TESLA cars and who knows, maybe he will even sell his saintly breath in hot air balloons. No wonder artificial intelligence is the next MAGA techi new thing; there ain't no real intelligence left.

Now the latest news from the charming duo. I'm ignoring Bounce; he is busy attending concerts at the Kennedy Center and waving to crowds of loving admirers. He wears earplugs to deaden the overwhelming approvals of programming by MAGA.

The oracle on high has delivered another proclamation that Canada should become the 51st state. (Maybe the United States should consider becoming a province of Canada—wasn't that the issue during the war of 1812?) Taking over Greenland is still being verbalized, and it's looking quite certain that China will be required to cede their territorial interest in the Panama canal and if not, invasion plans are underway. Meanwhile, the stock market dropped another 537 points today, reducing all American's 401Ks and Smell's taxable income significantly.

Enough of my bite-your-tongue remarks. The good news is Americans are waking up. Protesting crowds grow larger; resistors speak out more frequently; judges rule against MAGA routinely with accompanying scathing opinions; and TESLA is inching toward bankruptcy. Hold your breath— Republicans and Democrats alike may choose to host a third impeachment trial instead of being voted out of office themselves by the public.

Not Backing Down

In the 1960s, protests swept through colleges, universities, and some high schools and churches. Marchers filled streets and freeways of America, carrying signs, chanting slogans, and singing songs of freedom. When destinations were reached, speakers of every stripe—remember Dr. Benjamin Spock, Mohammed Ali, the Chicago Seven, and John Lennon—spoke out, sometimes at great cost to themselves. Protestors were called communists, traitors, cowards, weaklings, homosexuals, outside agitators, foreign agents, and a host of other names meant to drown out the protest message. Racists had a heyday vilifying the Black Panthers and green card farmworkers. Speakers were arrested, jailed, and sometimes killed.

Americans generally believe in truth and decency. When our basic truths and civility are compromised, we feel violated. Underlying protestors' issues of the 1960s was the recognition that ruling politicians, Democrats and Republicans alike, were lying. History is being repeated.

Mass protests are happening again. The perpetrators of lies have recognizable identities—oligarchs and knee-jerk politicians, paroled January 6 insurrectionists, DOGE bullies and cult worshippers of MAGA. What is different this time is protestors come from all levels of American society. The underlying issues—lying, cheating and exploitation—are the same. Sound familiar?

Fired government workers, retirees and pensioners, 401K investors and small businesses, veterans and probationary hires, young, middle aged and older people, males, females, and LGBTQs, college-educated and school dropouts, are today's 'long hairs' of the past. However, we are no longer allowing ourselves to be emasculated as members of the hippie counter culture; now we are members of the dominant culture.

A social revolution is taking place. People are standing up for their rights--democrats and even a few republicans, independents, and non-political citizens—are not backing down. Take note Republican hide-a-ways and timid Democrats, **we are not backing down**! Lead, follow, or get out of the way.

Liberty Bell

In 1947, the Liberty Bell was put on a train and toured around the continental United States, stopping in over 300 communities. My northern Minnesota town was one of those. The Second World War had recently ended, and our 1st and 2nd grade teacher, Mrs. Paulson, spent several lesson hours explaining the meaning of liberty and the sacrifices millions of soldiers had made to ensure that we kept it. There was a crack in the bell from over-exuberant ringing, but its meaning was clear, sacrifices are required to protect our liberties.

Possibly at no time since that bell rolled into my hometown, Bemidji, Minnesota, have our liberties been more threatened. A demented elected politician countenanced the attempted violent overthrow of our government on January 6, 2021, and pardoned its perpetrators. Twice impeached, 34 times convicted, but re-elected four years later, he is now destroying the American government from within.

Operating personnel are being fired, physical assets sold, financing appropriations rescinded, domestic and international contracts and treaty agreements cancelled, and, in the words Steve Bannon, he us 'visiting all holy hell on those who oppose him.'

Meanwhile, his MAGA cult members, Republican acolytes, wishfully aggrieved supporters, and innumerable felonious compatriots cheer him on and celebrate the destruction he is wreaking, lovingly caressing their weapons while anticipating the Armageddon they longed for.

But another crack is forming, this time not in the bell of liberty but in the gongs of destruction. The American public is rising up, resisting, opposing, and rejecting the agents of doom. Their voices are being heard, lawsuits are being won, and Democrat-led town halls—no longer the favorite prerogative of right wing provocateurs—are extinguishing the Republican mantra of greed and self-righteousness.

Democratic politicians should take careful notice. As the evil MAGA empire crashes, the mantle of refurbishment will not fall to an acquiescent or compliant replacement. Adherence to the past is being rejected. More of the same under a different administration will be swept into oblivion along with the maniacal T-party destroyers of the present. Now is the time to conceive of, articulate, and then secure, a principled rebirth of OUR DEMOCRACY.

Not Stupid

Several MAGA cult members have objected to being called 'stupid' because they voted for the man who identifies himself as our current president (or King). 'Stupid' is a very direct, descriptive term that might describe voting for a person who claimed he would be a dictator on the first day. The word is abrupt and carries a connotation of not being very smart. The vote wasn't very smart, but who knows about the voter—s/he may have been a successful billionaire, a Republican congress person, an uninformed first time voter, or even a disgruntled former democrat.

The person might have been overwhelmed by $250 million sponsorship of right wing propaganda or may have listened only to FOX news stories. Maybe that voter was in extended mourning for Rush Limbaugh or even is a sorry loser in the affluent economy and reached out for any lifesaver within reach. Stereotypes and expletives don't work well when describing voters because there are so many different varieties, motivations, and who knows, maybe even counterfeited votes (Trump did say the election was rigged.)

Consider the word, 'stupid.' It is blunt, may be used as a term of disrespect, implies a lack of intelligence, often is a visceral response, is easily dismissed as imprecise, cannot be directly measured, and might better be represented by any number of synonyms: brainless, silly, unintelligent, or irrational (e.g. see synonyms in Microsoft Word).

Words such as dumb, idiotic, daft, empty headed, thoughtless, misguided, wasteful, reckless, rash, dangerous, unwise, and foolish might substitute, but they are somewhat tame for a serious endeavor like voting for president of the United States. It's hard to find a word in the English language that conveys the same impact as 'stupid,' but perhaps a modifier helps: 'incredibly stupid." Ok, enough already. I'm sure you get my point.

Waiting--by I. L. Kafka

An old man stares through a rain-streaked unwashed window.

His clothes are worn, shabby, thread bare.

Inside is a dirty, dusty desk.

A pen with leaked ink stained the surface.

It has lain unused for years on the desktop.

A uniform hangs on the back of an unstable wooden chair.

The shoulders show S.S. on each sleeve.

DOGE is written across the back of the garment.

Shiny, black boots are on the floor.

A cap with MAGA written on it is on the table.

Knee length trousers complete the discarded wardrobe.

"Oh, dear, look at that poor man," the woman says as she and her escort hurry along the sidewalk toward their waiting car."

"Yes, love, we are in the old government section of town. It is shut down now, mostly deserted. Only a few stragglers are left. Hurry. We don't want to be late."

The entry door has occluded wavy glass.

It is lettered with 'Social Security Office. Enter.'

The door is locked.

No one is inside.

An empty cabinet door swings freely.

Rat droppings are on the floor.

"That man looks familiar. Don't we know him?" she asks.

"No, I don't think so. We don't associate with people like that."

"He looks like old Mr. Weir. But he died years ago, from malnutrition, I heard."

'Yes, he did. He couldn't collect his Social Security benefits anymore."

"Well, then, who is that? He looks like our former neighbor."

"It's his son. He's waiting to get Social Security Survivors Benefits."

"Oh, so sad. I should give him a dollar."

"No. We don't want to encourage people like that. Come along, Mel. Our limousine is waiting."

The man, not old at all, didn't hear their words.

He had been deaf from childhood.

He stared through the window.

He was waiting for the office to reopen.

Note: Kafka's stories were written in short, stochastic sentences, imbued with irony and alienation. Even in translation, his words are poignant and direct. Although imitated (including my feeble attempt) no writer has been able to emulate Kafka's style. It's fun to try, though.

What are democratic values?

We can start with life, liberty, and the pursuit of happiness.

Freedom

Fairness

Equality

Inclusion

Authenticity

Civility

Humaneness, and many, many more.

Values don't have to be inclusive of one another, and they don't have to be exclusive either. They do have to be universal for all people. 'Of the people, by the people, for the people' is one expression of the need for universality of values.

Most of all, values must be internalized—that is, people must believe in them, and a majority of people must sincerely be willing to act on them. Without application, values are empty promises and lies.

In many ways, a nation is identified by its leaders' portrayal of its values. Are you happy with MAGA representation of American values?

Lucky are the Already Dead

Lucky are the already dead who have no eyes to see the maimed bodies in the rubble.

… who have no ears to hear the screams of babies and cries of mothers.

… who have no smell of the decaying bodies and burning flesh.

… who have no mouths to gasp for air in the vacuum of an exploded bomb.

… who have no tongues to taste the burning sulfur on their family's bodies.

… who have no sound to scream in pain for those who cannot.

… who have no words to tell of the crimes of war.

… who have no voice to condemn the guilty who stand by and watch.

… who have no minds to understand the horror of each day's terrors.

… who have no conscience to suffer hell on earth.

… who have no children to ask why.

Lucky are the already dead who have no need to hide from the everyday shame of their continuing silence.

Note: Netanyahu's genocide in Gaza continues without more than a whimper from us. We should all be ashamed.

Genocide

Last night, on national television, Senator Schumer excused killing 400 more women and children, bombing more schools and hospitals, and exterminating thousands of Palestinians by claiming there were Hamas terrorists hiding among them. Genocide is never excusable, no matter who commits it.

Bruised

I am bruised. I keep pinching myself to wake up from the nightmare and find I am already awake only living in the Trump world.

Bob Dylan once wrote (my paraphrase), 'Sometimes I think the whole world is one big prison yard where some of us are prisoners and the rest of us are guards.'

I no longer care which side of the bars I am on so long as it is not on the MAGA side.

Ponzi Schemes

Nolite te bastardes carborundorum—a fictitious phrase from *The Handmaid's Tale* meaning 'Don't let the bastards grind you down.' Musk calls retirement accounts, Social Security, 401-Ks, and Medicare payments Ponzi schemes.

Waste, Fraud and Abuse

Representative Julie Fedorchak, Senator John Hoeven, and Senator Kevin Cramer of North Dakota, you should convene *face-to-face* town halls immediately to explain your support of President Trump and Elon Musk's activities aimed at closing Post Offices, Veteran's Affairs offices and Social Security offices and firing personnel from each. Soon during the runup to the next election you three members of Congress will see your faces on NOT WANTED posters, to wit:

NOT WANTED Representative WASTEful Fedorchak,

NOT WANTED Senator FRAUDulent Hoeven, and

NOT WANTED Senator ABUSIve Cramer.

These posters will appear in every Post Office, Veterans Affairs office, and Social Security office in North Dakota. If the trend catches on, you will see them paraded outside schools, libraries, and airports. Buttons with your NOT WANTED faces will be distributed widely. Furloughed mail people, veterans with disabilities and grade school children will have NOT WANTED pictures of you on their empty mail bags, roadside wheelchairs, and bookless backpacks.

Hand lettered signs will be featured in dozens of protest marches that are occurring every weekend in North Dakota. Seniors like me will tell their children, grandchildren, in laws and friends to never vote for any of you. You will soon learn the real meaning of RECALL, IMPEACH and VOTE OUT. My advice: pay attention. We are.

Dinosaur Relics

Congresswoman, please don't fall for it! Don't conduct a fake 'telephone town hall' pretending it is the real thing. Don't insult your constituents, your voters, and yourself by debasing them with a phony stab at transparency when both you and they know the actual reason is to hide from the controversies caused by two fakers in the White House and their two senate acolytes from North Dakota (three if you count the former governor).

Instead, Congresswoman, meet the occasion directly with honesty and courage. Rent the largest venue available, get up on the stage and take the heat. Tell your supporters and opponents exactly what you believe. Tell them what you don't believe and tell them why they should accept your view of what is good for North Dakota.

Of course there will be cheers and jeers, laughter and boos, acceptance, and rejection. That is what town halls are for—to allow an exchange of ideas, feelings, and sentiments. Stay on that stage until the end, until the last person has spoken. Let protestors and attestors have their say. When it is all over you will have something your upper chamber colleagues will never have, respect from your audience and most importantly respect for yourself.

Sixty-five years ago, a young woman, a 15 year old teenager, got up on a stage, faced a crowd and sang her song. With a few words, she captured her audience and all of America. The musician was Brenda Lee. Her words were:

I'm sorry, so sorry

That I was such a fool…

_____

I'm sorry, so sorry.

Please accept my apology…

You're not a fool, Congresswoman, but your Republican MAGA colleagues are. Comparatively speaking, you are a young legislator, embarking on your first term. Don't let relics from the past drag you into their mire. Stand up for yourself and stand up for North Dakota.

Note: This Post was written before the newly elected Congresswoman from North Dakota had cast a single vote.

Watching

"The whole world is watching," chanted demonstrators, "The whole world is watching!" Chicago police waded into the crowd swinging their batons, grabbing the hair of girls and hirsute men to inflict as much pain as possible. Activists and uninvolved bystanders were forced into busses and vans for transport to hastily assembled concentration camps. Clouds of tear gas rose above the boulevards reflecting the flash of exploding cannisters. Bright television lights illuminated the violence and obscenity orchestrated by the reigning mayor of America's host city to the Democratic National Convention.

One or two delegates inside the pavilion expressed horror and anger at the carnage taking place outside. They too were hustled out of sight. On camera, commentators tried to mitigate the violation of democracy with 'This is shameful,' some finding good people on both sides of the conflict. While the protest movement was driven toward the dark recesses of the city park, hand-picked delegates nominated their best man to carry the Democrat's flag. He lost.

By only a slight margin, less than half a percentage point, the joyful warrior was vanquished by soon to be America's first nationally disgraced politician of modern times. Out of the desert of ignominy the Republican standard bearer entranced the 'great silent majority' to support a lost war in Asia and reject the voices of their children, the protestors at Grant Park in Chicago.

America's continued dissolution, begun by Nixon and now in full force under Trump, bewilders democratic politicians and astonished international leaders. They stare dumbly at what once was a powerful country built on the rule of law crumbling before their eyes. Planeloads of hastily gathered brown faces are shipped off to penal camps reminiscent of the death camps of Hitler and the gulags of Stalin. Pairs of thugs dressed in the militaristic garb of commandos force short-shackled captives into transport planes. Upon arrival, their heads are shaved; their humiliation is meant to bully the remaining populace into acquiescence and submission.

Maximum visual effort is employed to terrorize white and non-white Americans alike with 'We will come after you wherever you may be.' Their words, uttered by a venomous designee of the most evil cadre ever to inhabit the upper levels of American government, are gleefully repeated by right wing media dupes. Oligarchic billionaires funnel millions into willing acolytes' election coffers.

The whole world is watching. We are horrified by the fall of what once was a "great shining city on the hill." Criminals are pardoned and the rule of law is ignored. Unelected and elected tyrants brag while gutless Republican enablers cheer violators to evermore offenses. A few citizen objectors are hustled off to jail, while multitudes of resistors gather in front of campaign offices, court houses, jails, and town halls. Their signs, banners, flags, and voices are rising. Soon, while the whole world is watching, the evil MAGA empire will come crumbling down. The whole world is watching.

Speak of the Devil

Well, Congresswoman, how did it go? Was your 'telephone town hall' successful? Were you, as written by Rudyard Kipling in 1895, able to "keep your head when all about you are losing theirs and blaming it on you?" Were you able not to be an insult to your constituents, your voters and yourself when you defended Mr. Trump with 'He is only doing what he was elected to do?' Please pardon my boldness for asking, but you got more votes than my preferred candidate, and because I live in North Dakota, you now are my representative in Congress too. I must ask.

You see, Congresswoman, I am really bothered by what is happening to our government and our country. I grew up in a farm family that only could afford one new shirt and one pair of pants each year for me in the fall when school started. Nevertheless, the United States of America of my youth promised a better future even if the present wasn't all that good.

Promises, Congresswoman, are what got you elected to the House of Representatives. All first time elections are good faith events, where voters believe the promises of their candidates. After that, all elections are based on 'promises kept.' Will you be able to keep your promises, Ms. Congresswoman?

I apologize for leaning toward over-dramatization. Early in life, I began to read epic poems and listen to grand operas. In Die Walkure, Amazonian-like female gods galloped across the sky, reaching down to snatch the souls of dead heroes which they devoured to enhance their power over the earth. King Lear, Othello, and Hamlet are plays about man's internal struggle between good and evil, right, and wrong, decency and vileness.

Shakespeare is great, but I believe Goethe's Faust best describes the conundrum in which you now find yourself. Faust sold his soul to the devil in return for earthly fame, power, comfort, and riches. Afterwards, the devil came to collect. Your devil is the one I am referring to.

I understand your dilemma, Congresswoman. You are trapped (entranced?) by a group of GOP-MAGA oligarchs who retain their power by preying on the souls of young newly elected congress people. These oligarchs aren't going to give up their position of wealth, but they will attempt to buy your soul. They will force you to realize their promises, not your own. It is the only way they can retain power over people they dehumanize daily by intimidation, threats, lies, deportations, robbery, cheating, physical violations, demeaning, and other forms of cruelty.

Who owns your soul, Congresswoman, you, or the devils who court you?

Cabinet Meetings

I'm watching Trump's Cabinet Meeting! Even he must be embarrassed by the drivel these people are spouting. I think unprintable words while Attorney General Pam Bondi's is talking.

Say What?
Recognize, resist, and impeach!

Democrat's Task

The task of becoming an elected Democrat is to be able to articulate a better solution to America's problems than Trump's MAGA, DOGE, and ICE are proclaiming. As Walter Mondale asked years ago, "Where's the beef?"

This Will Not End Well

Nightmares and premonitions interrupt my sleep. I awaken, fearing some lunatic with a gun has slaughtered dozens of people in misguided rage against MAGA resistors or insane support of MAGA promoters. Some heroic DOGE-MAGA bomber was going to detonate a IED device hoping to close down a meeting of protestors in middle America. Another January 6 attempt to overthrow the government would accomplish the hanging some imagined MAGA enemy. More trucks plowed through crowds of innocent children. This couldn't happen; I had to wake up.

I dream something more stupid than rounding up immigrants and shipping them to foreign countries will happen. Accusations of treason against former presidents will be made. Federal funds to research institutions will be rescinded. Maybe national vaccination projects will be cancelled triggering new covid and measles pandemics.

Millions of foreign workers will be repatriated to their home countries causing a labor depression in the US. International graduate students will be grabbed off the streets and disappeared by gangs of thugs claiming to be MAGA-DOGE operatives. Tariffs will be randomly applied to imported goods resulting in a world-wide economic trade war. Economies will collapse. This dream has to be a nightmare.

In my awakened state, I regain my rationality. Only an insensitive political idiot would threaten Social Security, take health care away from millions of people, attack law firms and judges, and shut down support agencies for veterans and people with disabilities. Who knows, feeling protected by a Supreme Court ruling that a sitting president can do no wrong, only a clinically insane person would attempt to fulfill his boast and shoot someone on the streets of Manhattan. This couldn't really happen, could it?

Reviewing my nightmare scenario, I remember dreaming that war plans were leaked to a national news agency not yet subdued by the MAGA government. An attention-hungry president contemplated sending troops to the Canadian border, annexing Greenland, invading Mexico, and taking it upon his own recognizance to send American soldiers to war. Seeking a Nobel Peace Prize, the demented president kowtowed to a petty Russian maniac. Nothing, it seemed in my bad dream, was beyond possibility with this crazed head of state.

I remember thinking this will not end well.

American Gestapo

During my interrogation they asked me why I did it. Why did I speak out, poke my stick at the Russian bear, scream epithets against the American bombs, voice my chagrin at the genocide in Gaza, protest the MAGA-ICE kidnappings of students and non-white men?

"You are an old man," they said as if they needed to remind me, "who had no reason to jeopardize your comfortable life, your retirement, your home, your standing in your community, and your family. Why did you speak out against us?"

I mumble a few incoherent words. I am exhausted. I don't sleep at night. Each time I hear a car door slam, or a dog bark, or a branch blowing in the wind rattle a window, I wake up. At every noise, I anticipate their battering ram smashing through my door.

"Speak up," my inquisitor demands.

I drove to the grocery store and stopped for a red light. In front of me was a police car. In the lanes on both sides were men staring straight ahead pretending not to be watching me. Behind me followed a car to close for me to escape. 'Is this where I will be taken,' I thought, 'abducted off the street?'

"Don't be ridiculous," my interrogator said. "There were too many bystanders who might have complained had we arrested you at the traffic stop."

At the store, I had carefully chosen my aisles so as to not be trapped by 'clerks' pushing empty produce carts, approaching me from both ends.

Should I topple shelves of canned goods, give a token resistance by throwing some eggs at them? Should I run?

"That would have been infantile and futile," he says.

But at least I wouldn't have gone quietly. I would have given a few seconds of token resistance.

"Token, but for what end? There were five of us. We have guns, handcuffs, batons, and pepper spray. What would you have accomplished? Become a martyr? Why?"

I believe him. That's how they took the young Turkish woman student off the street. Five masked agents kidnapped her in plain sight, zip locked her wrists and hustled her out of the state against a federal judge's orders. Where is she now? Are they breaking her body as they have destroyed her life? Is she among the felons, rapists, 'worst-of-the-worst' they grabbed a week earlier? Physical violation is what they understand. Is she now the revenge toy of villains?

"Why?" he shouts at me again. He wants a reaction, an answer, something to validate his existence.

I would have kept some of my dignity, I thought. I wouldn't have been a wimp, had I resisted.

"For the last time, tell us why you opposed us." The self-appointed inspector general got up from his chair. "Tell us why?"

"Because" I scream at him, "I am ashamed to be silent!"

I don't feel the bullet that scrambles my brain, blows out my tongue, and silences me forever. I never hear them say, 'We were only following orders.'

Dead Men Walking, and Walking Dead

Two phrases from earlier years aptly describe the circumstances in which we now find ourselves— Dead Men Walking, and Walking Dead.

Lawyers, college presidents, foreign students, government employees, errant journalists, even two or three dissident Republicans are Dead Men Walking. Whether they acknowledge their impending fate or not, they are scheduled for extraction and extinction by the MAGA machine.

Many will be furloughed by their organizations who are afraid of sanctions by the ruling regime. Some will be deported, have their visas cancelled, or be 'disappeared.' Reduction in force will be the reason many are placed on unemployment rosters.

The most egregious among us will find ourselves without livelihoods or resources to fight our economic and social dissolution. The publicly courageous—those whose stand was acknowledged to be bold and daring—will find their applause meters resting at zero. This is ominous but not devastating.

More ominous and edging America toward national devastation is the presence of the Walking Dead. The Walking Dead are all the members of Congress and political operatives who at every level of government are afraid to exercise their sworn oath to uphold the Constitution of the United States. It is they who have condemned themselves and us to a dying democracy. They are the Walking Dead because there is no evidence that they have working brains, hearts that beat, or eyes that see.

Nothing passes as intelligence in these automatons. Complicit members of the Walking Dead are the mindless enforcers commissioned by MAGA, DOGE and ICE. Their eventual defense, 'I was only following orders,' echo the sounds of their Nuremberg ancestors.

Remember *Fahrenheit 451*? It is the temperature at which banned books burn. There are only a few degrees left before the American Constitution is to be fed to the fires of hate, revenge, greed, and dominion.

Ashes to ashes, dust to dust.

Sunday Sermon: It is Intentional

"We hold these truths to be self-evident...Life, Liberty and the pursuit of Happiness." This one sentence in the Declaration of Independence is the strength of and basis for American democracy. To destroy American democracy, truth must be destroyed. Alternative facts, multitudes of lies, student extractions and expulsions, economic marginalization, elective disenfranchisement—these are the enemies of truth.

For the oligarchs, dictators, and overlords, 'truth' is the most dangerous word in the English language. Destruction of 'truth' is the reason why elected rulers lie, dictators imprison, violators rape, and killers murder.

Babies are born into life. Their little arms and legs move and grow with abandon and liberty. Their giggles and faces emit happiness. Women endure the pains of childbirth to perpetuate the joy of children.

It is not accidental that women and children are dragged by their hair to become captives in dark Gaza tunnels. It is not accidental that babies and children are relocated to distant Russian cities away from their homes. It is not accidental that the greatest number of bombing casualties in wars are women and children.

Killing women and children in Gaza and Ukraine is not accidental, it is intentional. The maiming, disfigurement, and deaths of women and children with bullets, missiles and bombs are intentional. The intention is to eliminate the bearers and living embodiments of truth, to eliminate truth itself.

By destroying truth, rulers, dictators, violators, exterminators, and killers have their way. It is the death of American democracy. It is intentional, and silence--our silence--is complicity.

Sounds of Silence

Do you listen carefully to hear the screams of children under the rubble in Gaza? Do the dying gasps of women pinned to the kitchen floor by beams fallen from bombs in Ukraine provide cocktail conversations for you? Is the unaided earthquake devastation in Mandalay music to your ears? Is it your nationalistic desire to crumble the towers of academia to rid the United States of DEI and Foreign Student competition? Is your political and patriotic philosophy to 'break a few things' so that they can be put back together in your preferred way? Do you wear the hat proclaiming MAGA? Is this how you propose to make America great again?

We are in the midst of revolutionary times. Wars abroad and wars at home, threats of annexations and deployment of forces to destabilized borders, kidnappings, and deportations—these are the headlines that dominate the news. The prevailing logo of our times is MAGA—Trump's red hat proclaiming he is the only one that can Make America Great Again.

So far, all Trump has managed is to Make A Great Ass of the United States. We've become the horror and laughing stock of the world. MAGA has earned an international reputation of Madness And Greedy Acquisition. Meaningless Actions Gone Awry is another way of construing Trump's expressed ambitions toward Greenland, Canada, and Panama.

Were our armed forces not the most powerful in the world, Trump's infantile behaviors would merely be a bad joke. Unfortunately, with Hegseth, Musk, Rubio, and Bondi in place to support the man who would be King, the joke's on us. Nobody is laughing.

Creative Non-Violence

The National Guard was called to protect the campus at Berkeley from anticipated threats from hordes of hippies, freaks, long hairs, commie sympathizers, and draft dodgers. In short, war resisters. The year was 1969.

Thousands gathered outside Sather Gate, an ornate iron edifice that marked the end of Telegraph Avenue and the entrance to the University of California's Sproul Plaza. A few years earlier, it was the site of the Free Speech Movement. Down the street was a vacant lot that later became People's Park. It was a warm, sunny day. A day for Creative Non-Violence.

Creative non-violence doesn't require blood, guns, or destruction. These are the tools of villains, felons, and election usurpers. Creative non-violence doesn't require millions of dollars, bought and paid for presidencies, coercion of lawyers and election officials, nor faked town halls to deliver   failing messages to DOGE. There is no need for burning and keying of Tesla's, splashing paint on showroom windows or throwing rocks at policemen. Violence only begets more violence, prison sentences and fines, and sympathy for the oligarchs who would betray America.

Inside Sather Gate, National Guardsmen stood at attention, rifles pointed toward the sky at 45 degrees. Protestors sang, 'All we are saying... Is give peace a chance.' Words decorating tye-dyed T-shirts advised 'Make Love, Not War.'

A young woman standing near a rigid immobile soldier took a flower from her hair and placed it in the muzzle of his gun. A photojournalist filmed the event and found his picture published everywhere. One flower, one picture, one song showed the world the power of Creative Non-Violence.

Creative non-violence only requires People to stand up for what is Right and raise their Voices until the din of destruction is lost in the rebirth of Democracy. The year is 2025.

El Teatro Campesino

It was more than an organizing tactic for the United Farm Workers Union. The El Teatro Campesino theater troupe traveled the backroads of California's central San Joaquin Valley to perform for farm workers in the fields, churches, back yards, barely sustainable hovels, Quinceanera celebrations, Saturday nights and Sunday mornings, anytime, anywhere. The theater group was created, led, produced, directed, and acted in by Luis Valdez, a Chicano dramatic genius who also authored an epic poem called *I Am Joaquin*.

Their stage was the flatbed of a truck. El Teatro Campesino performances brought heart and hope to Hispanic green card holders, naturalized Mexican American citizens, imported 'wet backs,' hungry undocumented illegals, and lowly paid refugees from everywhere. Together with Cesar Chavez, Delores Huerta, several organizing 'recruits' and California Rural Legal Assistance lawyers, El Teatro Campesino helped energize a disenfranchised group of Hispanic people into a proud cultural movement called La Raza.

Chicano power became the face of the United Farmworkers Union. It was the triumph of Ghandi-inspired non-violent methods used to win battles with lettuce and grape growers. Chavez spoke and fasted. Huerta became a political force of reckoning. Valdez spread the word to a population outside the mainstream of communication. CRLA attorneys represented impoverished clients in court. Membership in the union grew. National attention was garnered.

La Raza again finds itself under siege, this time from union busters, haters of DEI, and DOGE-ICE gendarmes. Legitimate and undocumented Hispanic citizens are being harassed, kidnapped, and deported to alien destinations. Families are broken up, student visas cancelled, false charges levied, court rulings and appearances ignored, and illegal imprisonments regarded as normal. Repatriation to hostile homelands is administered without paying attention to the danger foisted on political refugees.

What will happen? Will a new El Teatro Campesino be formed? Will another Cesar Chavez emerge from a traumatized and beleaguered Hispanic population? How long will non-violent resistance be used to right perceived wrongs? Will the fastest-growing minority populations in the United States remain peaceful? Will the newly named Gulf of America be returned to its original Gulf of Mexico title together with land areas of Texas, New Mexico, California, and Utah? Will a more perfect union not include Trump, Musk, pardoned January 6 felons, Republican enablers, and DOGE henchmen?

Robert Roark, speaking of the Mau Mau revolution years ago, said 'when you take away the values of a people, you reap the whirlwind.' The winds of change are blowing.

The Dignity of Labor

A few years ago, Jeremy Rifkin warned in the *End of Work* of a future imbued with technology created mass unemployment. Recently, one of the top ten richest men in the world predicted artificial intelligence (AI) will reduce work life to a two day week. Other commentators and academics have raised alarm of a takeover of world economies by monolithic corporations that control the wealth of nations by acquiring ownership of the means of production and control of the distribution of goods.

Fears of robotic devices capturing people's jobs are predictions of dire employment futures. Defenders of employment rights are regaled as anathemas by capitalist overlords.

Unless they have venom dripping from their lips, speakers who utter words like 'dignity of labor,' 'humane work conditions' and 'socialist' are themselves vilified in language and action. Conservatives celebrate an Orwellian twist to the meaning of 'right to work' with the argument that unions are promoters of unfair work rules and union organizers are communists and 'outside agitators.'

The convenience of online encyclopedias lead students to believe they no longer have to learn how to think. Ignorance is celebrated as godliness. Complaints of new math and individualized learning haunt public schoolboard meetings. Righteous disputations involve intense discussions about book banning in schools and public libraries. Lies and false equivalencies are heralded as alternative facts.

This is the Brave New World of the Maga Republican cult of Trump.

Into this fray of prophetic confusion comes a savior of mankind, a genius of wealth creation, an end war on the first day Nobel Prize aspirant, a Make American Great Again prophet, and the solver of all problems great and small. Behold and bow down in awe to our next Mount Rushmore visage, the exalted President Donald Trump!

President Trump claims to have saved America from itself. Tens of thousands of government employees have been fired. Billions of dollars funding health and food programs for people at home and abroad are cancelled. DEI pollution of the arts and literature is being excised from national museums and buildings. America's premier performing arts venue, the Kennedy Center, has a new leader, Donald Trump himself. Rapists, convicts, felons in chains (except himself and January 6 acolytes) and all shades of non-white people have been forced into off shore prisons.

And now, best of all, Americans who are no longer assured access to Social Security, Medicare, Medicaid, and FEMA can rejoice in a plunging stock market and expurgation of their retirement savings by the wonderful imposition of the largest tax increase the United States has ever seen, just announced by President Donald J. Trump on April 2, 2025. Tariffs for everything. Aren't you glad for everyone who voted for him!

Note: It should be observed that after Trump reneged on his tariff proposal earning him the acronym of TACO—Trump Always Chickens Out--, the stock market recovered, but not until two trillion dollars' worth of damage had been done to retirement funds. Wall street brokers had a heyday.

The Last Day

Sunshine, melting snow, and budding apple trees. What more promise is there for a summer of love? Today is April 5, 2025--the last day of my 83rd year. For all that time, for better and for worse, it has been my honor to be an American, to feel happy that we were compassionate, generous, fair, and strong. It was my privilege to walk among people who were smarter and stronger than me, and whom I could count upon to lend a hand when a hand was needed. I never doubted the goodness of the America I lived in when there were some events and some people's actions, even some of my own, that I regretted.

It's hard not to blame, not to take a self-righteous approach to the goofiness and nuttiness and utter stupidity that characterizes our current American president. He and his Republican acolytes are attempting to tear our country apart, but we cannot let them divide us in two. Unity is our strength, division our demise. Many of the marchers and protesters today will carry a banner, Indivisible.

I like to think togetherness is the solution for overcoming the forces that would have it otherwise. Even in the worst of times we have revealed ourselves in our best light. Today is a bright day. As the song goes, 'Just call my name, I'll be there'.

Note: This post was written the morning before I attended a well-attended protest march on the Veterans Memorial Bridge spanning the Red River of the North between Fargo and Moorhead.

The First Amendment

"Congress shall make no law respecting an establishment of religion or prohibiting the free exercise thereof; or abridging the freedom of speech, or of the press; or the right of the people peaceably to assemble, and to petition the Government for a redress of grievances."

Citizens assembled five deep the total length of Veteran's Memorial Bridge across the Red River of the North holding signs indicating "Hands Off" of our constitutionally guaranteed rights. Our chant, 'This is what democracy looks like,' rippled up and down the rows of protestors that lined both sides of the bridge as a steady stream of like-minded automobile riders traveled between North Dakota and Minnesota, honking horns and gesturing their approvals as demonstrators called for an end of the Trump reign of terror.

Messages and mottoes were handwritten on thousands of garage and kitchen-made placards, some on small pieces of cardboard and others on great unfurling flags in the breeze. Taken in totality, the signboards documented the multitude of offenses against the people of the United States of America. Still other notices decried the travesties being hurled at other nations—Canada, Ukraine, Mexico, European countries, and even islands without inhabitants. The presence of people who are veterans, students, retirees, LGBTQs, old, young, rich, poor, male, female, small and large indicated a broadly based rejection of the DOGE, MAGA, and Republican acolyte destroyers of America.

There was more, so much more. The turnout made April 5, 2025, one of the most memorable days of my lifetime. It is an honor to have been part of a truly patriotic expression of America's promise and greatness.

Peace Be With You

Several weeks ago I began publishing short essays on Face Book to express my chagrin about travesties being laid upon us by the Musk/Trump presidency. The story I told in the first essay concerned volunteer Peace Corps nurses working with the World Health Organization and USAID. These nurses traveled over nearly impassible Afghan mountain passes to villages that had never seen a Westerner before to administer smallpox inoculations. Their combined effort was nearly 100% effective but required vigilance to insure continued success in defeating this dreaded disease. Now Trump has withdrawn the United States from WHO and cancelled USAID worldwide. The Peace Corps funding is in danger. Smallpox is again killing people.

Stories about Peace Corps successes are remembered by every one of the 240,000 PC volunteers who served since the program began in 1964. Most stories involve small things—a kid who learned his first English word, help for a woman whose baby almost died, men who were shown a more efficient way to irrigate a field. Occasionally a major story about a canyon bridge connecting two remote villages or an organized collective of women empowered to sell their cottage industry goods in an international market is heralded by news media. They are stories to us, but important and unforgettable lifesaving events for people in the host countries.

Returned Peace Corps volunteers are found throughout the United States. Several have been elected to Congress, many teach and do research in American universities, and some have become major players in the business world. A large number continued their international work through non-government organizations, a few joined the State department, and former volunteers can be found running charities and service organizations in most cities and rural areas of the United States. Their service to America lasts throughout their lives.

DOGE has now decided to visit the Peace Corps headquarters in Washington, D.C. I would like to believe the Musk storm troopers would recognize an inherent value in having worldwide ambassadors fostering good will and aid to third-world countries but given their treatment of other US assistance groups my confidence is blown. It appears DOGE is only motivated by jealousy, vanity, and lust.

Based on past performance, the Musk/Trump presidency's only reward is destruction of whatever can be found that was good and ennobling from earlier American endeavors. Unable to produce any positive results themselves, they are determined to tear apart every good thing that preceded them.

Trump/Musk/DOGE/MAGA must be stopped. Election of a Wisconsin judge, the speech by Cory Booker, and the nationwide protests of April 5 are a good beginning. As those thousands of Peace Corps volunteers have proven, success comes with one small smile at a time. More nonviolent protests, election organizing, programs of action, targeted boycotts, neighborhood gatherings and meetings, support for afflicted workers, law suits, and information campaigns are needed. Intelligent and purposeful resistance to build a movement that will overcome the MAGA destroyers is our way forward. George Washington overcame winter weather, lost battles, insufficient resources, hunger, and disease to gain a Nation. We can do it too.

Trumpian Economics

Donald Trump has accomplished two almost impossible feats this past week. First, he diverted attention away from two losing wars and the kidnapping of several men off the streets of America and turned attention of the visit of the chief proponent of genocide, Benjamin Netanyahu, into a yawning event given the enormity of the failing economies around the world.

Understandably, people whose life savings, rent monies, retirement, social security, health insurance and food allowances are being zeroed out do not have a lot of time to worry about Trump tariffs.

Secondly, Trump economics is helping the megarich solve one of their most perplexing problems, how to dispose of all their surplus money before the taxman requires them relinquish a small part to the government coffers. There is nothing the rich hate more than paying their fair share of taxes.

'The Donald' in his infinite wisdom has come up with an ingenious solution—make the money disappear. Caymen Islands, Swiss banks, revocable trusts—awe, those are old style diversions. We have to think modern. He, himself, has made money he owes disappear six or seven times through clever utilization of bankruptcy courts. The fact that his contractors, creditors, and American banks lost their money as well didn't faze him—presumably they had a surplus money problem too which he erased.

The Case of the Disappearing Money will undoubtedly become an Agatha Christie style book and movie. We know who the Director is. Currently starring are Bezos, Zuckerberg, and Musk with cameos by several Trump cabinet members.

Whether the plot involves high crimes and misdemeanors, or merely felonious thefts is yet to be worked out. Stay tuned.

Note: Trump's great accomplishment was to create a two trillion dollar stock market crash. See the following post.

When the Bough Breaks

Rock a bye baby on the tree top,
When the wind blows the cradle will rock,
When the bough breaks the cradle will fall,
And down will come baby, cradle and all.

He gave them just enough time to unload their personal stock before the threat of tariffs drove the market into free fall, causing investors large and small to panic and create a selling spree. Down, down, down went the market.

Brokerage houses, FOX News commentators, and insider oligarchs loved it. Traders are paid fees as the market goes up and traders are paid fees as the market goes down. Commentators keep their jobs by spouting even more outrageous lies than emanate from the White House, and oligarchs move swiftly to capitalize on any bit of information privately spread through their network of in-the-know compatriots. They, too, get paid when the market moves, especially when they are alerted before it happens.

Desperate world leaders, not knowing what insane actions were next to unfold, did their best to assure their citizens they were on top of it. Messages, enquiries, and pleas were sent to the Man in the Florida White House. He gloated, wrote his oracles from on high, and played golf. Hints, surreptitious phone calls, and outright guffaws accompanied notices of impending 'face-saving' change.

Ostensibly, the turnabout occurred because major Oriental countries began to unload their treasury bonds, telegraphing they had lost faith in the safety of holding America's debt. Panicked, presidential advisors shouted out in the middle of the night the tariffs must be lifted. Uncertainty and pleas moved even the most dogmatic and authoritarian of rulers.

According to liberals, he buckled. According to Republican acolytes, he made a masterful move in the Make America Great Again game. According to Wall Street traders, he rescued us from cataclysmic losses. (Of course, they didn't return any of the fees they charged for selling out their investors nor the fees they charged for buying back the stock they sold at a much diminished prices!) The oligarchs—they kept the faith in their religious investment dictum: buy low, sell high. The fat cats just got fatter. Thankyou Mr. President.

The Devil is in the Details

North Dakota Congresswoman, I apologize for repeating myself, but I wrote the words below several weeks ago when you were still an untainted new legislator embarking on your journey as a national representative.

"I believe Goethe's Faust best describes the conundrum in which you now find yourself. Faust sold his soul to the devil in return for earthly fame, power, comfort, and riches. Afterwards, the devil came to collect. You know the devil I am referring to." (Quoted from my earlier post.)

In spite of the company you keep--that is, I felt I couldn't blame you for your two depraved senate colleagues who were elected by the people of North Dakota, not by you--I wrote a plea for compassion. I really felt you had an opportunity to be a person of consequence, someone who valued decency and honor above the vanity and decadence that your upper chamber colleagues revere.

Stupid me! Here you are avoiding town halls, spouting the MAGA line, genuflecting to the rich and infamous, and LAST NIGHT, casting a vote to impoverish older people, take away health benefits from veterans and people with disabilities, bankrupt Social Security, kidnap immigrants, etc.

Congresswoman, you crossed the line. Last night's VOTE recorded in your name will stay with you forever in the Federal Register. Not only will future opponents use it against you in campaigns, but this vote will become part of your permanent legacy of SHAME. It is a small detail in the stupendous villainy of the MAGA regime, but it is your detail, Congresswoman, and the devil will be back to collect again and again and again. Even Faust could not defeat shame. Can you?

Kill All of the Lawyers

The Trump Administration clearly has a problem with federal court lawyers, and he is working to rectify it. The evidence is abundant.

Early in his first Presidency, Trump ran into trouble with Attorney General Jeff Sessions. Even though proving his dislike for civil rights and civil liberties, Sessions showed that he had a spine after all when he wouldn't bend to Trump's wish to be absolved of allowing the Russians to mettle in the presidential election. Bye-bye Jeff.

Let's leap over the dozens of law suits that Trump lost (all but one) on his way to overthrow the elective will of the people (Jan. 6) and ignore the later spectacular civil court losses to women he offended resulting in awards of many millions of dollars, most of which he is still trying to weasel out of. Instead, consider the tenaciousness of his present endeavors.

With the gratuitous help of Senator Mitch McConnell, Trump has managed to pack the Supreme Court with acolytes who will bend over backwards to 'make legal' his insane actions. Disappearing immigrants, quashing official secrets lawsuits, absolving armed thugs of Capitol assaults, and alleged traitorous behaviors are among his every day pursuits. His MAGA-minded Supreme Court has ruled Trump can do no wrong while he is President.

As he can, Trump fired his predecessor's appointments whose mandate was to adhere to the rule of law in the United States. Then he attacked judges he doesn't like. (Was his own sister one of them?) Several of his attorneys didn't quite meet the muster, so adios. He installed a complaisant politician as Attorney General who is gutting the Justice Department of specialized and career attorneys. Their offense, it seems, is 1) adherence to the law, 2) competence, and 3) expertise, and 4) failure to adequately oppose Donald Trump's losing lawsuits. If you can't 'Leap tall buildings at a single bound' you're out.

His stellar achievement is cowing the legal profession—represented by some of the biggest and most lucrative law firms in the world—into submission and fear. Prestigious firms who previously claimed to wantonly represent the least among us grovel at Trump's feet. Bribes of millions of dollars' worth of pro bono services are offered to Trump if he will merely look the other way. What courageous people to be so brave!

While he is President, the most powerful man in the world is bent on avenging past wrongs. After brushing up on his high school Shakespeare class, Trump discovered a henchman's solution to our legal barriers, "The first thing we do, let's kill all the lawyers."

Using this literary precedent as an excuse to persecute real and imagined enemies is a little farfetched, but convenient. Maybe Trump's next move will be to shoot someone on Fifth Avenue. Do you think?

The Democratic Experiment

In law a man is guilty when
He violates the rights of others.
In ethics, he is guilty if he
Only thinks of doing so.
--Immanuel Kant

For several hundred years, clerics and philosophers concerned themselves with understanding both mental and physical behavior. Their motivations were conditioned by the sense that for there to be better relations among people there had to be better relationships within people.

Early philosophers were interested in how values shaped behavior and character, and how to incorporate those values into the formation of a just society. Commitment to reasoning and self-examination were considered essential virtues, not only for one's self but as guides for teaching children.

As divergent world views began to dominate the consciousness of mankind, the concepts of right and wrong and of guilt and amelioration were introduced as mechanisms to govern personal and social conduct. Adherence to the distinctions of right and wrong became foundations for law, and guilt and redemption became the canon of morality.

A new social order achieved preeminence in the seventeenth and eighteenth centuries with the founding of democratic societies. In America, legal and religious forces advanced along two parallel tracks, both dependent upon the will of the people.

For nearly 250 years the United States increased its societal well-being by adhering to the rule of law while subscribing to inherent values of life,

120

liberty, and the pursuit of happiness. When disruptions occurred, they were settled by legal challenges and through the value influences of community based on shared morality.

The strength of our nation grew along with its standing among peoples of the world. Although only a few countries sought to emulate the United States of America, all took into account its enviable status as a democratic nation based on legal and ethical principles.

A revolution is taking place that proposes to destroy the American way of life. Persons guaranteed due process by the Constitution are taken off the streets and disappeared into foreign prisons. Government organizations are attacked and their employees forced out of jobs by self-appointed regulators. Courts are complaisant or their rulings ignored. Citizens who protest are threatened with incarceration and/or expulsion. Neither legal nor social morality prevails.

We are now faced with a predicament. How can the violation of the rights of others be stopped so we can better think of ourselves as free from the guilt of destroying of what is unique in America, its values, and its rule of law?

Nightmare in White

My eyes opened to a white room. The walls and ceiling were white.

I sat at a white table, in a white chair. The table and chair were fastened to the white floor.

On the other side of the table was a high stool, its circular cushioned seat also white. It was not fastened to the floor.

I was dressed in a white canvas smock, open at the back. Long arm crossed sleeves were tied at the back. I could not move.

I was dressed in no other clothes. My feet and legs were bare. The room was cold.

My head was shaved.

A large window glass was occluded with a white fog. Shadows moved on the other side.

Muffled sounds percussed the glass as occasional laughter erupted. The room was deathly silent.

Seconds, minutes, or hours passed before a white person came into the room.

The person was dressed in white. Her hair was white, straight, long. Her polished nails were white.

She sat on the white stool, smoothing her white uniform over her white stocking covered legs. Her shoes were white.

"Why are you here?" she asked with an unaccented white voice.

"I don't know. I was walking my dog when two huge men forced me into a white van. I don't remember anything else. I was given something from a syringe."

Her lips were pale, straight. Her teeth were white.

"Why are you here?" she asked again.

"I don't know," I said. "My dog didn't pee or defecate on the clean white street. I can think of no reason."

Muted laughter was heard from beyond the whitened glass. She moved her head from side to side very slightly. The laughter stopped.

"Why are you here?" she asked for the third time. Her voice was flat, not kind or unkind. Only slightly insistent.

I answered in Spanish, my native language.

"No se. No tengo ni idea, Senora."

The white woman nodded, got up from the white stool, and exited the room through the white door. Only white noise remained as evidence she had been there. The shadows moved away from the white, fogged glass.

Now I knew why I was there.

Paranoia

"Are you awake, now?" the young therapist asked.

"Yes, I think so. My head is groggy. Why are my wrists tied to the bed?"

"You were hallucinating; we gave you a sedative to calm you down. You are restrained to keep you from harming yourself."

"Could I have some water?" he asked. She held the glass with a straw up to his face for him to drink.

"Can you tell me what made you so frightened?" she asked.

"My bad dreams," he said. "I haven't slept well for months."

"Describe your dreams for me," she said.

His face registered thought, concern, and fright.

"The first dreams I remember involved being at protest marches and being grabbed by men who forced me into their van. They had masks over their faces. Their actions were always in slow motion. My friends reached out for me, but they couldn't hold on. I was taken away. I wasn't allowed to speak."

"Do you remember another dream?"

"After my first dream kept me awake for several weeks, they changed. I dreamed my head was shaved, my clothes had been exchanged for a white jump suit, and I was always looking through bars. It was noisy. I didn't understand because I don't speak Spanish."

"How long did that dream go on?"

"Days, weeks, months. I'm not sure. In my dream, my hair would grow out and my hair was cut again. I tried to talk to them, but they wouldn't listen."

"What caused you to become frightened?"

"I dreamed men with masks would come to our cell and take people away, one at a time. They never returned. New faces replaced the ones that were gone."

"And the release of some people made you afraid?"

"In my dream they weren't released; they were killed."

"And that dream caused you to believe you would be the next one to die?"

"No, I'm not afraid of dying. It is my last dream that terrorizes me."

"Can you tell me what that dream is?"

"In my last dream I see people being forced into vans. I observe them having their heads shaved. They stare out of prison cells. One by one they are taken away and not heard from again. I can't stand it anymore."

"Why is it so frightening?"

"Because it is me who is grabbing, shaving, imprisoning, and killing them! I am the masked man."

Stand Back and Stand By

Who are these DOGE/ICE marauders that grab people off the streets and 'disappear' them? Are they the convicted January 6 criminals with a new charge? Is overthrow of the most powerful country in the world as simple as that? Whoever would have thought it!

Future Prosecutions

I hope the laws that are being broken by MAGA/DOGE/ICE are recorded for future prosecutions.

Standing Up!

Keeping up with the MAGA/DOGE/ICE tragicomedy acts is not easy because there are so many of them. Yesterday it was refreshing to witness the acts of three Senators and a member of the House of Representatives having a positive effect.

One Senator admitted 'she is afraid; we all are afraid." Fear of losing America to the mob of right wing invaders can be a good fear—recognition is an early condition of resistance leading to change. Fear of the mob itself—well, I think caution is a better stance. Mobs such as MAGA/DOGE/ICE are energized by cowards. In the end they fail, and they run.

The second Senator, speaking together with the youngest elected Representative to Congress has warned for years of the malfeasance of oligarchs. Together, these two legislators are providing a popular face for the millions of ordinary citizens who are standing up against the tyranny of the MAGA right. Not only are they revealing the shame of Republican acolytes who refuse to meet with their constituents, but they are demonstrating that America can and does have better faces.

I personally admire most the Senator who absolutely refuses to abandon one of his constituents to the henchmen of evil. He is making good on his promise to represent and help a family victimized by ICE marauders in every way he can including travel to the El Salvadorean concentration camp imprisoning Kilmar Abrego Garcia. To date, this Senator's actions have yielded a hotel visit with Mr. Garcia. Although constructed as a sham by El Salvadore's dictator, the Senator's visit is having positive affects for the Garcia family and improving chances for Mr. Garcia's return to the freedom he deserves.

Resistance and persistence pays off, and those three Senators together with one Representative are to be commended. But further attention must be given. Oppressors often employ deception to mask their continuing violation of the rights of people everywhere. One man may be saved, but thousands are begging to follow. We must stand up for them too.

Note: Kilmar Abrego was a graduate student grabbed off the street by ICE thugs and sent to a El Salvadore prison without any legal deportation or criminal court procedures allowed. Several weeks later the social pressure succeeded to get Kilmar Abrego returned to the United States to fight the trumped up charges against him.

Veteran's Memorial Bridge

Over 500 people expressed their patriotism at Veterans Memorial Bridge in Fargo-Moorhead April 19, 2025, with messages written on handmade signs.

We gathered to protest MAGA/ICE/DOGE and JANUARY 6 Republican mistreatment of America. People of all ages were represented including post-retirement men and women, individuals who are middle aged, and even a few children and babies. Not missing from the group were Viet Nam, Iraq, and Afghanistan veterans.

The signs were colorful, informative, and direct. Some were symbolic, a few commercially printed, and ranged from small to large. Words copied from many of the signs are as follows:

WE ARE NOT BACKING DOWN!/ WE THE PEOPLE ARE UNDER ATTACK FROM THE TRUMP ADMINISTRATION / NO TAX CUTS FOR THE RICH/ LEAVE MY FINANCE ALONE/ WTF/ BRING ABREGO GARCIA HOME/ MY OPTIONS TRUMP THE TRUTH/ FU DT/PROTECT OUR CONSTITUTION/ IT'S NOT LEFT OR RIGHT, ITS RIGHT OR WRONG/ MELANIA, BLINK TWICE IF YOU NEED HELP/ NO KINGS!/ 6 MILLION $ FOR EL SALVADORE BUT 0 $ FOR SOCIAL SECURITY/ WE ARE ALL IN THIS TOGETHER/ RESIST FASCISM/ WE HAVE BRANCHES OF GOVERNMENT, NOT A KING/ PRO AMERICA, ANTI TRUMP/ DUE PROCESS/ CONGRESS DO YOUR JOB/ HANDS OFF MY USA/ GET IN TROUBLE, GOOD TROUBLE/ REPUBLICANS, TAKE OFF YOUR BLINDERS/ STOP PRETENDING THIS IS NORMAL/ HANDS OFF FREE SPEECH/ ...AND JUSTICE FOR ALL/ TRUMP HAS

DESTROYED OUR DEMOCRACY/ DEFEND OUR CONSTITUTION/ TRUMP SUCKING DOGES GO HOME/ GOVERNMENT FOR THE PEOPLE NOT SCREW THE PEOPLE/ REMOVE TRUMP NOW/NO!/ HELL NO TO PRIVATIZATION/ HANDS OFF OUR DEMOCRACY/ STAND UP CONGRESS/ GOP GROW A SPINE/ RESIST/ TIME TO SPRING CLEAN; AMERICA IS SMELLING MUSKY/ OF THE PEOPLE, FOR THE PEOPLE, BY THE PEOPLE/ HANDS OFF MEDICAID, MEDICARE, SOCIAL SECURITY/ SAVE US/HANDS OFF DEMOCRACY/I SPEAK FOR THE TREES: HANDS OFF OUR PUBLIC LANDS/NO KINGS: MUSK MUST GO/ 86 47/ MUSK=RAT/ IMMIGRANTS MAKE AMERICA GREAT/ STAND WITH UKRAINE/ FIGHTING OLIGARCHY/ HANDS OFF HEALTH CARE/ CANADA, GAZA, UKRAINE, GREENLAND, PANAMA/ MUSK IS THE IMMIGRANT WHO TOOK YOUR JOB/ FIGHT FOR THOSE WITHOUT YOUR PRIVILEGE/ WE, THE PEOPLE ALL NEED TO BE TREATED LIKE FELLOW HUMAN BEINGS.

The protestors were congenial and friendly with one another and waved to the occupants of automobiles that passed by. Drivers honked horns in support although two loud muffler vehicles raced by several times displaying middle finger salutes. Like most Republicans in Congress, they appeared not to be interested in expressing their views via an informal town hall meeting on the bridge.

Remediations

It's time for more action—specific remediations for MAGA/DOGE/ICE/January 6. Persist, Resist, and Rebel.

Redress

When will Protest become Redress? He's had his hundred days. Now, we'll have ours.

April 19, 2025

"A cry of defiance, not of fear."

No Explaining Wanted

Why do we ask MAGA/DOGE/ICE and their Republican acolytes to explain themselves? Is that not an act of indolence on our part? It's time to move on.

Trump's Feint

All across America and in several other parts of the world protestors against MAGA/DOGE/ICE and GOP chanted, held up signs, and 'witnessed' the human, political and domestic travesties being dumped upon them with uncanny speed and volume.

The 50501/Indivisible gatherings of April 19 like the confrontations several Saturdays before became the largest peaceful demonstrations of political resistance in modern American history. In any reasonable political environment legislators and administrators who are targets of those demonstrations would consider the scope of their activities to be sure they weren't negatively impacting the citizens they took an oath to defend.

MAGA/DOGE/ICE/GOP? No siree. The more people protest and the more people that protest the happier these groups of villains become. Breaking things, hurting people, trampling on civil rights are music to the ears of today's right wing political extremists. Joy in their world is made up of starving kids, destroying health care, inflicting humiliation, kidnapping immigrants, denying science, wrecking economies, and stealing from the poor to benefit the wealthy.

Faceless Republican legislators use diversions of our attention to pursue their primary objective, 'stealing from the poor to benefit the wealthy.' While conscientious Americans protest the illegal and inhumane treatment of Abrego Garcia, January 6 acolytes pass laws giving oligarchs the biggest tax break ever experienced paid for by working class Americans. Millions of people who juggle their weekly finances to provide food, clothing, health, and home for their kids now are expected to reward the wealthy with more of their earnings while receiving no benefits themselves.

It's a feint. We look one way, they plunder and steal from another. Our only certainty is while freedom allows them the opportunity to do wrong they will not stop. It's time for working class Americans to rise up and say "Stop! Your Time for Grift and Graft is Over." We don't want you, and we don't need you. Go back to your private islands and oceanside villas and get out of the way so we can clean up the stinking mess you have created. And by the way, we have enough prison cells in America for you too; you won't have to be hustled away to El Salvador.

An Addendum to Trump's Feint

The Democratic effort to win freedom for Abrego Garcia addresses AN important issue, but if Democrats myopically fixate on it as THE important issue, we will have already lost the next election, and as many more after as the MAGA/DOGE/ICE crowd can devise by singling out other individuals to trample on their rights.

Inclusion Not Exclusion

Percy Bysshe Shelley wrote, "If winter comes, can spring be far behind..." It's a good metaphor for the changing political seasons, especially this one. It's conventional for political advisors to caution Democrats to appeal to constituents' pocket books and self-interest, to engage us with 'bread and butter' issues, to abandon the Republican branded WOKE issues they claim are the bible of the left. I differ.

America's strength is built on values that argue for shared fairness, decency, equality, freedom and more for all, not just for the well-off or exceptionally lucky and powerful. During our developing history as a nation, we have always worked toward building a 'more perfect' union and not been satisfied to rest on the status quo.

The world-wide appeal of immigration to the United States has been 'I can be included too.' A nation that favors everyone, not the few will have more friends than enemies. The basis of the Republican anti-immigrationists demand is to maintain their own selfishness and parochialism. Democrats can do better and should.

As most Americans are, I am a proud descendant of immigrants. My Swedish-to-the-Red River Valley of the North ancestors worked hard not only to thrive and survive but to insure their neighbors and fellow Americans did the same. Their success was shared and passed on, not hoarded for a few. Their two-horse teams have become the mammoth tractors of the present, but the reason for using them is the same—to feed the world.

Selfishness and exclusion is not the American way,
democracy is.

Post Review

Based on a casual review of three months of Face Book Posts, nearly all agree MAGA/DOGE/ICE is the worst thing that has happened to America since the Civil War. So what do we do about it?

Recognition and Resistance are the first steps.

What's next?

Response: What to do is still beyond my grasp.

Reply: 1) Don't give up. 2) Don't give in. 3) Don't take any crap from them. 4) Don't despair; America is still a good place to live.

The good news is they are old, decrepit, and failing. MLK said (paraphrased) 'I've been to the Mountain Top. I may not get there with you, but I've seen the Promised Land. One day, we, as a People, will get there, together.' Believe him; I do.

State of the Union Update

Everything goes faster in Trump world. Well, his golf carts are slow, but they are built to carry a lot of weight. With lightning speed The Donald ended two wars. Putin's war in Ukraine, now under Trump's watch is an incursion not a Russian invasion, and Benjamin Netanyahu's devastation of Gaza has euphemistically evolved into a mop up action, not the genocidal war continuing to kill multitudes of women and children.

Of particular interest is the speed at which the United States government and U.S. Constitution are being shredded. Whole agencies waft away faster than quarks. Thousands of federal employees become permanent unpaid volunteers. A few high end law firms and universities sell out attempting to acquiesce to MAGA/DOGE/ICE demands. The emergency cases filed at midnight are inundated with obstruction of justice government lawyers babbling illegal nonsense in dragged out hearings that occur in remote jurisdictions with complaisant judges.

Trump's hit men and women have generated uncharacteristic government promptness in destroying the very agencies they claim to protect and administer. Mr. TESLA Musk's computer whizzes charge into buildings with algorithms of extinction, reminding us in cyber world nothing is ever lost. Privileged data is rendered inaccessible except to Musk's self-designated waste, fraud, and abuse crusaders.

Tom Holman of ICE fame has reappeared to send his masked vigilantes to invade borders, streets, colleges, churches, unlocked homes, day care centers and other venues that merit scrutiny. With Third Reich cum KKK echoes, fathers are wrenched from their families, graduate students are absented from their research, and non-white everybody's are removed from tattoo parlors. MAWA, Make America White Again, prevails.

Our wistful Appalachian Vice President proudly displays the Flag with his worldly travels. To date he has jetted off to Greenland, soon to be annexed. Canada is soon to become the 51st State. England had been Vance's destination, presumably to upgrade his genuflecting skills. He went to the Vatican to receive forgiveness for the sin of having only three children. Finally, he has traveled to India to beg for alms for the poor.

Is he learning Spanish to facilitate an invasion of Mexico? Busy man when he's not breaking trophies. Hopefully, he won't freeze when nominating his boss for Pope in the secrecy of the College of Cardinals. Dante would be delirious were he around and create a new circle of hell for all of Trump's people.

The ever-so-coifed Secretary of Defense cavalierly declassifies war plans to avoid running afoul of the Official Secrets Act when whispering to his wife, brother, and legal staff. RIF to him is firing generals, demoting highly valorous female officers, and locking out civilian functionaries who keep the place clean and running. No need for pilots when there are robots. Recruitment officials are unnecessary when college Republicans are available to fill the ranks. Now that we have very attentive satellite observers in the sky military intelligence units are obsolete and unnecessary.

Other cabinet luminaries have been diligently active as well. Pam Bondi journeyed to El Salvadore to strut in front of dehumanized men. She enunciated the new Trumpian rule of law—MAGA might makes imprisoning migrants right! Although 75% of the men behind Bondi had no criminal records, presumably before they reach old testament adulthood that omission will be rectified in the privacy of their cells.

Kristi Noem's prior job was shooting overly energetic South Dakota dogs while alienating the Governor's office from Native American tribes. Undoubtedly, knowing how to destroy an animal qualified her for the charge of keeping Americans and the rest of the world safe. According to Homeland Securities' Press Office, "her strong leadership insures that DHS is hard at work securing our borders, arresting and removing criminal aliens, safeguarding the U.S. cyber infrastructure, protecting America's leaders, deterring terrorism, and keeping America safe." Not to be outdone by Mr. Homan, she 'rides with ICE' on occasion to capture bad guys. She also wears a white hat.

Billionaire Doug Burgum, Secretary of Interior, is highly visible but not a highly vocal member of the Trump team. One sees him standing nearby eating hot cookies when another Executive Order is about to be memorialized. Mr. Burgum's 'craggy, western cowboy face' lends photogenic gravitas to Trump's pasty demeanor, so he is a welcomed addition to every signing occasion. Impressive events are in Burgum's future as coal-fired power again becomes king. 'Drill-baby-drill' resonates as the mantra of the capitalist right, and Earth Day and the New Green

Deal are soon to become nostalgic left-wing memories.

There are too many other Trump employees to cover adequately. One additional person bears mention. Chairman Jerome Powell, a major loser in Trump's eyes, has demonstrated grace, independence, competence, and patriotism uncommon among Republicans. Only Liz Cheney and Adam Kinzinger have attained the level of respect and honor due to Mr. Powell for his intransient determination not to grovel or succumb to presidential ignorance. Powell may be the only thing that saves the United States from complete economic disaster caused by Trump's tariffs. More power to him.

One can only hope.

Grasping at Straws

Maybe. Three events in the political landscape over the past week lead me to believe hope is not merely a wishful thought.

First, with a spoken sentence from Trump the stock and bond markets took a roller coaster ride. The economic turmoil wasn't an expression of disapproval for the random moves the Republicans are using to run the government. It was sheer terror and fear by the billionaire monied class that they were about to pay for their blind obedience and votes for a group of amateur politicians. Classic American capitalists love economic change when it involves their coming out on top or represents the fall into destitution of someone else, as long as it isn't their own downfall.

Associated with the erratic movement in the investment world was the news that TESLA earnings were down by 71% using conservative measures, and even more when the big picture of the company's remaining assets was taken into account. The decline wasn't only attributed to TESLA's faceless electric truck (remember EDSEL), but directly a result of the company's number one owner, Mr. Elon Musk.

Musk built his wealth and his company over a period of years (with some sweetheart contracts from the United States government). He destroyed a large part of his wealth and his company in a short period of months by demonstrating what a first class jerk he is. Along with him, he has tanked the political fortunes of Mr. Trump and the GOP. As Elon Musk exits U. S. government service, the neutering of

MAGA and DOGE will be recognized as his greatest achievement.

Second in my litany of blows against the MAGA/DOGE/ICE destruction machine are the opposition of Harvard and hundreds of other colleges and universities who are refusing to comply with invasive Trump edicts. Their resistance together with rulings by several judges reveal the illegality of government kidnappings. Finally, the singular actions of Senator Van Hollen have focused America's attention on the plight of one ICE victim. Together, all of these events are revealing that our would-be-emperor has no clothes.

Third (and very proudly I am happy to point out), significant resistance has developed and is growing in all 50 states and territories. Throughout the world resistance against illegal and immoral dereliction of duty employed by Trump and acolytes has mushroomed.

For several weeks and especially over two Saturdays in April 2025, millions of protesters have carried banners and signs, paraded across bridges and college squares, shouted questions in actual and facsimile town halls, written polemics and social media posts exposing the violations of right wing zealots. All made their message loud and clear—STOP MAGA/DOGE/ICE & TRUMP NOW!

Impeachment and conviction is not out of the question. The cracks and crumbling of the Republican dream were not caused by Democrats, protesters, nor victims. MAGA/DOGE/ICE are the instrument of their own downfall. Musk, not consumers, destroyed his wealth and company. The illegal activities of Tom Homan and Trump

Republican acolytes have prompted lawsuits. Protestors exposed themselves to cold, rain and snow, hot sun, and lost weekends because of Trump-Musk-Homan threats, not because it was a convenient way to waste time.

In America, even good can be a result of bad faith.

96, 97,98...

It's not exactly a milestone one would wish to celebrate except that President Trump, Elon Musk and Tom Homan weren't allowed to do more harm than they did.

Franklin Delano Roosevelt set the hundred day standard with imaginative and experimental programs that demonstrated through the New Deal that government could be used to benefit a majority of people. Among Roosevelt's legislative accomplishments were the Agricultural Adjustment Administration (AAA), National Industrial Recovery Act (NIRA), Tennessee Valley Authority (TVA) and the Civilian Conservation Corps (CCC).

These and other endeavors had an over-arching goal of bringing the United States out of the Great Depression by employing millions of jobless people. Additional programs included the Federal Securities Act (FSA was later enhanced by the Securities and Exchange Commission SEC), and the Glass-Steagall Banking Reform Act supplemented by the Federal Deposit Insurance Corporation (FDIC) that protected depositors from loss when banks failed.

The most impressive accomplishment of the Roosevelt era, produced not by the four-term president but through the organizational efforts of his widow, Eleanor Roosevelt, is the Universal Declaration of Human Rights, adopted by the General Assembly of the United Nations in 1948.

The atrocities of World War II were forerunners of many events occurring in Gaza and Ukraine today. The cumulative effects of that world upheaval were so terrible countries sought to articulate an ideology that would prohibit such offenses against humanity from happening again. The compelling thought was that human rights should be protected as a rule of law. The Declaration of Human Rights contains thirty Articles, ranging from statements of personal status—"All humans are born free and equal…" to "No one shall be held in slavery or servitude…"

Article 5 is particularly applicable in this time of jailing people in El Salvador's maximum security prison. It reads, "No one shall be subjected to torture or to cruel, inhuman or degrading treatment or punishment."

Articles that Messrs. Trump, Homan, and Musk might pay particular attention to are Article 7—"All are equal before the law…", Article 9—"No one shall be subjected to arbitrary arrest, detention or exile," and Article 14—"Everyone has the right to seek and to enjoy in other countries asylum from persecution." Ms. Bondi, please take notice.

It is increasingly apparent that the American public, joined by leaders and people in many other countries, have rejected the MAGA/DOGE/ICE philosophy of destruction. Trump poll numbers are dropping precipitously; agencies and institutions are refusing to be bullied; huge demonstrations in every state and community are expressing unmistakable opposition; and lawyers and judges are beating back the offenses embodied in the President's daily Executive Orders.

There are more battles to be fought, wins and losses to come, but the tide has turned. America will survive. MAGA/DOGE/ICE won't.

Perhaps She is Right

Several days ago I promised myself to stop inserting hate speech in my Posts. It's not easy given the MAGA/DOGE/ICE people are such inviting targets. I found myself morphing into their image. Camus once observed, 'he who commits his last ounce of energy to pushing a rock up a mountain becomes the rock himself.' I have no greater horror than becoming one of the MAGA acolyte crowd.

It's not easy. Passing through FOX propaganda (be careful!) channels on the way to an old movie exposes me to a lunatic (opps!), vacuous (shut my mouth!), incredibly stupid (hate the sin, not the sinner!), slimy (now you've done it!) utterances of a ridiculous (close to the line!) Pam Bondi (don't write it, you can be sued for licentious language!).

Each time this person (aha, a gender-neutral word!) opens her glistening mouth (what does that mean, she uses lip gloss?) she emits hurtful (well, sometimes truth hurts), snarling, venomous (hmm, haven't used that phrase before!), vindictive (get off it, it's the law!), racist (absolutely not!), unkind (now that's better!) words that mean absolutely nothing (come on, so she's not a linguist!).

Undoubtedly, Attorney General Bondi feels she is being forceful, direct, and honest in the light of the removal, deportation, and incarceration efforts undertaken by her operatives. She is doing the job her boss says he was elected to do. She speaks with his authority. She is held in awe by the other members of his Cabinet team. Nearly all elected GOP legislators are silent while her voice and actions command the town square. The MAGA/DOGE/ICE and January 6 pardonees applaud her efforts. Cowing law firms, imprisoning judges, and disappearing children works for Republican voters, so perhaps she is right.

When judgement day comes, Bondi and all the other Cabinet members will argue, 'please excuse us, we were only following orders.' They will beg forgiveness from the children, fathers and mothers, non-white immigrants, international graduate students, street strollers, lawyers, and judges, etc. who became recipients of the MAGA-ICE way.

Hopefully, all of these people will not remember the hate words I am trying to extinguish from my vocabulary when they call the Trumpies to account for what they have done to America. They trust we will respond with American kindness...will we?

Embarrassed

I'm a little embarrassed. Anything I write about MAGA/DOGE/ICE criminal activities is tame compared to what is daily reportage on the World Wide Web. Citizens everywhere know the truth and are not afraid to say it. Even in spite of threats of arrest from Pam Bondi for speaking out, Americans are telling the Trump administrators of terror they won't take it anymore.

My mother used to tell us as squabbling kids 'if you can't speak nicely about one another, don't say anything at all.' Her's was an enforceable direction. Mothers sure know how to reduce an assembly of complainers into silence. Will I ever be able to raise my voice again?

Impeach and Arrest

Impeach him and arrest them. Do something!

Above the Law

"No one is above the law" spoken by Pam Bondi.

One Day Soon

One day soon we hope, North Dakota will become a bipartisan state sans Cramer and Hoeven. Our newest House representative is young enough to broaden her horizons although whether she will exercise her intelligence or not remains to be seen. Town Halls, even without our elected legislative representatives, are an exercise of democracy. Thank you for having them.

Note: This was a reaction to another writer's post declaiming the depravity of North Dakota's legislative contingent.

Shameful All The Way

The end of Trump's first hundred days is no different than its beginning, and every day in between. It has been shameful all the way. He began by pardoning his January 6 insurrectionists, astounded us with appointments of billionaires to his Cabinet, and left the world aghast by staffing the muscle of American government with dangerously mediocre administrators.

Through executive orders, Trump is destroying science, education, health, civility, and the rule of law. What used to be a social safety net is being systematically dismantled. He has completed his hundred days of infamy by kidnapping men, women, children, and babies off the street to exile them to death houses in other countries.

America's symbol of justice used to be a statue of a blindfolded Lady Justice holding a scale in one hand and a sword in the other. It was a pledge and a warning. Together with the Statue of Liberty, Lady Justice proclaimed we are a nation of laws and social fairness for all without fear of reprisal and persecution by the state. Living under the rule of law and order brought hope to millions fleeing an unjust world of dictators, strongmen, autocrats, and oligarchs. Not anymore.

America's vengeful voice now rattles the world with the venomous hateful words of Ms. Pam Bondi: "We will seek you out. We will find you. We will prosecute you. We will jail you. You will not escape our [concept of] justice." Under her (and ICE) direction, televised masked hoodlums grab immigrants, students, terrified women and children, lawyers, and now judges to be hustled away to distant airfields for the short ride to 'disappeared' oblivion.

The rule of Bondi/Trump law has become the rule of racists, crooks, insider traders, convicted felons, liars and cheats, corrupted elections and a Republican-led government dedicated to enriching oligarchs.

Historically, people such as Trump, Musk, Vance, Hegseth, Bondi, and Homan don't win. Like Hitler, they finalize their years in dugouts contemplating a martyr's end to their villainy. Some slink away to live out their glory days on small islands, others find prison cells to tap out messages to one another about their crimes. Thankfully, most are lost to the annals of history as soon as their fifteen minutes is over. With this promise, Mr. Trump's first hundred day reign of ignorance and terror ends. There will be more bad days to come, but we—the United States of America-- will survive them as well.

What Will We Tell Our Grandchildren?

The shame is mine, too. I am ashamed that I did not do more to stem the tide of Trumpism. I know I could have spoken more loudly. Maybe I still can.

Republicans are trapped. Their leaders are destroying people, government, and democracy. Daily offenses grow, and as obscenely bad as the first one hundred days have been, there are more bad days to come. By design or fate Republicans elect and feel powerless to intervene.

Of all those Republicans, only two were willing to relinquish political status and immediate power for future honor and a clear conscience. As Cheney and Kinzinger showed, honesty and resistance require brave choices and brave choices have costs.

Republicans who might have chosen to reject his tyranny at the time now are trapped between Trump's threats and their own electoral oblivion assured by the apparent collapse of the evil regime. Worse for them, as Liz Cheney pointed out, those Republicans who refused to certify Biden's election will forever be branded with the cowardly stance they pursued. There will be no profiles in courage stories written about them. What will they tell their grandchildren?

What will we all tell our grandchildren? I hope we can say that in the face of insidious MAGA destruction we did more than protest in the streets, town halls and public events, and during our Sunday morning absolutions.

My wish is to say we spoke up for unfortunate immigrants, students, mothers, and children, and even law offenders who were exiled from our American freedoms and possibilities.

I want our grandchildren to know we worked for candidates who opposed those who violated their oath of office and the rule of law in United States of America. I expect to say we found people who through their honesty and decency, were willing and able to reject the destruction caused by MAGA/DOGE and ICE.

I want our direct action to have mitigated some of the shame we all bear for allowing an oligarch to threaten American democracy. Most of all, I want to say truthfully we forged a better world for our kids than the one Trump and his Republican followers planned for them.

Madness in Great Ones

Many writers in the news feed still don't recognize the madness and irrationality of Donald J. Trump. They continue to speak of and about him as if he is capable of understanding reason.

Even as early as his first term in office, psychologists and psychiatrists warned we had elected a seriously deranged person who posed a danger to himself and all others within his sphere of influence. Although his spoken words and actions have only subjugated a few thousand people, he is becoming more erratic and dangerous by the day. It is time for the nation to take serious measures to mitigate the harm this mentally deranged President is causing.

It is obvious neither Mr. Trump's cabinet officers nor the Republican congress are going to fulfill their constitutional duty in this time of peril. Many of them—Pete Hegseth, Pam Bondi and Marjorie Taylor Green come to mind—are so consumed by fantasies of self-importance and greed not to mention cowardice and fear that they too are incapable of rational behavior.

One university, Harvard, and a few law firms have stood up to the MAGA/DOGE/ICE bullies but theirs is a lonely task. A few Democratic congress people have made valiant gestures, but long speeches do not provide sufficient opposition to masked kidnappers and home destroyers.

To date, several state and federal judges have been able to offer judicial curtailment of the ICE mobsters who assault citizens and non-citizens alike in the middle of the night. However, judges cannot act in a vacuum—the offenders must be arrested and brought before a court.

Laws are being broken. State's attorney generals can obtain warrants for their arrest, and sheriffs can bring suspected lawbreakers to jail. The public, as repeatedly shown by daily and weekly demonstrations across the country, will support ameliorative actions when they occur. Even though the lower level culprits are not giving the orders, it is their responsibility to abide by the law. Our responsibility is to hold them accountable when they do not. Without enablers, Trump's powers will become moot. My proof: notice how Musk's influence is collapsing along with TESLA.

Accomplishments

Nearly all Presidents have done something wrong, but only one President has done everything wrong. Likewise, nearly all Presidents have done something good, but only one President has done nothing good.

Franklin Delano Roosevelt created the New Deal that brought the United States out of the Great Depression. President Truman established the Marshall Plan to rebuild a devastated Europe. Dwight Eisenhower won World War II and created the Interstate Highway System. John F. Kennedy captured America's attention with a pledge to take a man to the moon and back and established the Peace Corps. Lyndon Johnson promoted the Great Society and became a champion of Civil Rights laws. Richard Nixon developed a lasting peaceful relationship with China. Gerald Ford helped the country believe in itself again. Both Jimmy Carter and Bill Clinton proved that a President out of office can perform national and international public services that win the respect of the world.

Even Ronald Reagan sounded like a statesman with "Tear down this wall!" George Bush the Elder asserted America's international status by promoting an expansion of NATO and a new world order, and George Bush the Younger's greatest moment was an enlightened program to save Africa from the scourge of AIDS with research and medicine. Barak Obama rescued the American economy and generated unprecedented prosperity while establishing a national health care policy. President Joe Biden saved millions of lives around the world with an intelligent quarantine and promotion and distribution of Covid 19 vaccines.

Heretofore, the American presidency was the envy of world leaders, respected and admired regardless of its occupant. "The President of the United States," were words everyone wished to be close enough to hear and tell their grandchildren about without embarrassment. Sadly, that is no longer possible.

Are YOU not ashamed?

The Ballad of Reading Gaol was written by Oscar Wilde following his own two-year imprisonment for 'gross indecency' with other men. While Wilde was incarcerated, a hanging execution of a man who killed his wife, "the poor dead woman whom he loved, and murdered in her bed" occurred.

After Wilde's release, he published the *Ballad* from exile in France, never returning to his country of origin. England, through its draconian homophobic laws, had stolen two years from his life and broken his spirit. To this day, Oscar Wilde ranks as one of the three or four best writers England has ever produced.

Wilde used the telling of the execution to illuminate the inhuman psychological conditions forced upon any prisoners of the State, regardless of whether they are innocent or guilty of the crimes for which they were convicted. He wrote, "I know not if the laws be right or if the laws be wrong, I only know in Reading Gaol the prison walls are strong."

In concise, lyrical verse, Wilde takes the reader behind the bars to feel the injustice all prisoners know, the insult of the restricted cells, the inhumanity of the guards, the memories of freedom before confinement, and the complete stifling of the soul, the terror and release through compulsory death. "I never saw a man who looked with such a wistful eye, Upon that little tent of blue we prisoners call the sky."

Imagine the humiliation, the withering of the soul, the pain of injustice felt by the prisoners in Louisiana, El Salvador, and other jails around the world being utilized by ICE. Many immigrants have no idea they broke any American laws, even if they did.

If reports are correct, few ICE prisoners will ever see the sky during their dreary days and nights. Their food would not even be used to feed barn animals, and their crowded conditions does not allow them even the slightest chance of rest or privacy. They are allowed no contact with the outside world, no letters, no relative's calls or access to lawyers. All that they are allowed to know is that the prison walls are strong.

The United States used to be regarded as the last, best hope for democracy, freedom, and the rule of law. People from around the world came here expecting fair treatment, hoping to build a better life for themselves and their children, and to escape intolerable conditions elsewhere.

No longer. We have become a Nation ruled by vain, selfish, cruel, and evil politicians. As a Nation, we embrace state sponsored terrorism, kill civilians, and imagined enemies with abandon, and offer hypocritical defenses for the worst tyrants the world has ever seen. We no longer live in a country of promise. Our society is characterized by greed, illegality, lies and selfishness.

WE are guilty because THEY are allowed to commit these CRIMES in our name. Are YOU not ashamed?

Dark Scary Words

Unable to defend the Trump tariff ideas, a southern Republican senator deflected a reporter's question with the words, 'Sounds like a question a communist would ask!' and moved on to a less intimidating FOX interrogator. Other damning words this senator often prefers to use to denigrate those he disagrees with are 'socialist,' 'Marxist,' and 'terrorist.' "It's socialism!" and "It's communism!" are among his favorite condemnations.

I wondered what fears cause this aged, grown man to be so vituperative in his responses to an inquisitive reporter's questions? Is there something about 'ist' and 'ism' that leads otherwise grownup people to react so fearfully?

A Google search revealed the word 'communisme' originated in France about 1841 and was used to indicate community and cooperation. Communal living became a popular form of raising young people in Israel and was adopted by some as an alternative life style during the heyday of the counter culture in the 1960s. Their hope was to increase mutual benefit accruing from sharing experiences, material well-being, labor, culture, and financial arrangements. Even birthing and raising children was shared in some instances.

Red flags (no pun intended) appear to be raised by 'financial' and 'birthing' aka sex. Both have their roots in sharing. Sharing of resources as a function of social arrangements quickly earn the harshly voiced characterization as 'socialism,' believed to be a close relative of 'communism' by many Republicans. Communal responsibilities for raising

167

children implies possible sharing of procreative tasks, a hysterical anathema among dedicated and devout (but not wholly asexual) Christian politicians. Financial sharing as a mechanism of society is largely accomplished through taxation, and that is positively no-no among dogmatic believers of stringent capitalism.

My three year old daughter used to love a picture book called *Who's Afraid of the Dark?* Together at bedtime, we looked behind curtains, under beds, inside closets, and in dark corners hoping not to find scary, frightening ghosts and goblins. When the night was dark and storms raged outside, pictures and words implied tremulous, threatening, evil outcomes that fortunately never materialized. I think, more than any other, that book instructed my daughter she didn't have to be afraid of words, doomsday visions, or verbal threats.

America needs to get beyond the dark 'ism' and 'ist' nomenclature to deal with reality. We do not have to be afraid of the dark.

Honor the Legacy

In 1962, President John F. Kennedy instructed Sargeant Shriver to proceed with the design and implementation of the Peace Corps which had three goals. Unpaid volunteers were recruited to 1) help countries interested in meeting their need for trained people, 2) to help promote a better understanding of Americans on the part of the people served, and 3) to help promote a better understanding of other peoples on the part of Americans.

At little cost, each of these goals has been achieved. The Peace Corps is a lasting legacy of the Kennedy presidency and has continuously engendered good will for America around the world for over sixty years. Returned volunteers live in every state. They work in universities, colleges, and schools, and many continue to serve their country in leadership roles in industry and government.

During these times of retrenchment and budget retractions, the viability of the Peace Corps is threatened. Members of Congress—especially those who find limited value in international good will and cooperation—need to be reminded about what the Peace Corps has accomplished for the world and America. The House of Representatives needs to support the Peace Corps' funding line in the current funding bill. (A personal note: I in Afghanistan, my step son in Kenya, and his son currently in Guinea have all served as Peace Corps volunteers.)

One Small Step

Together with millions of other Americans, I read about the travesties Trump and his Republican governmental acolytes are visiting on the United States and our allies around the world. Daily, the offenses pile up, no longer shocking to us but reducing our sensibilities to exclamations of horror and disdain.

In our most dreadful nightmares, we could not conjure a worser group of people to have power over our country. What about Hitler, Stalin, Netanyahu, Pol Pot, and the other villains of modern history, you may ask? Well, yes, they've killed more people and have earned their rightful place in genocidal hell, but that does not excuse us from responsibility for what is happening right before our eyes.

Astonishment leads us to claim, 'We voted for change, but we never voted for this!' Hand wringing, self-recriminations and faux guilt keep us following the lemmings off the cliff. MAGA aficionados laugh and cheer as we democrats, liberals, and persons laying claim to a sense of decency contribute through our own timidity to the destruction of America.

Hearings, disclosures, media dumps, texts, pictures, testimonials, leaks, revelations, exposes, evidences, testaments, shocks, investigations, considerations, scrutiny's, inspections, examinations, etc. of MAGA, DOGE, ICE and Trump's Republican acolytes and administrators are all necessary and represent small steps for mankind, but until a slew of MAGA, DOGE and ICE offenders are put in jail for their actions the small steps will be washed away like footprints in the ocean's sand. Legality and following the rules of law need not reduce us to impotence.

Aggressive actions—like publicly associating the culprits with their offenses and prosecuting them—must be pursued in every court in the country. Kicking a few Republicans out of office is titillating but imagine how more refreshing it would be to witness more 'perp walks'! Remember when we saw Trump hauled into court and found guilty for violating women?

American law, represented by Lady Justice holding a sword in one hand and a balance scale in the other, is being violated in ways that are equally important to address. It is time for these usurpers to be held to account! Renovating Alcatraz may not be such a bad idea after all.

Brain Damaged

When I was young, I ran into a swing. At the very instant of contact, I felt an excruciating pain, then nothing. I only remember the instant of contact, not anything else. My parents thought I was dead, but doctors revived me. I've lived with a three year old's memory of a terrible pain and a crease in my forehead ever since.

I wonder, now over eighty years later, if I was not administered a blow that resulted in a late-surfacing brain jolts, scheduled to appear only during times of extreme mental disturbance. Is it possible that my traumatic experience directs my mind away from understanding the painfully chaotic world around us in order to survive another day? From the day of the swing onward, have I been protected from absorbing indefensible shocks by an unconscious process of dissociation from the true meaningful impact of reality?

When I awaken in the morning I read that another eighty women and children have been killed by Netanyahu's bombing of a suspected Hamas hideout in a school. Putin refuses to attend a sit-down with Zelenskyy to 'talk' about ending the slaughter in Ukraine. Trump regards a $400 million airplane bribe as the 'art of the deal.' Although millions of Americans are threatened by floods and tornadoes DOGE cancels FEMA funding. The Republicans in Congress vote to pass a tax bill rewarding billionaires while taking away health insurance from low income Americans. The lead story in the news stream heaps accolades on a prominent Hollywood celebrity for wearing transparent clothing. Just another morning coffee review of world events.

Am I mad? These stories can't be true! Is this normal for American lives, an everyday morning coffee read out of world events? Is my addled brain protecting me from the realization that this reality is where I now live? Is there an explanation why I have no recognition, compassion, outrage, rejection of the violations being imposed upon my mind daily?

I look around me to assure myself I'm not a hallucinating vegetable presence imagining the worst possible world from my swing-shocked bed where I have lain for these eighty years. It must be all a horribly bad dream!

Nope. Innocents die, politicians prevaricate, leaders lie, disasters occur, charlatans steal, the richest get richer and no one seems to care. The little boy who shouts, "The Emperor has no clothes!" is confined to a hospital bed, unable to speak the obvious. This will not end well.

Ghosts

In Shakespeare's plays, ghosts are often employed to articulate "morality, duty, reputation and hypocrisy." The ghost tells Hamlet to seek vengeance for his father's murder but not to blame his complicit mother. A ghost leaves Macbeth with a guilty conscience to haunt him to his demise. "The evil that men do lives after them; the good is often interred with their bones,' says Mark Antony eulogizing the memory of Julius Caesar while condemning Brutus and Cassius for Caesar's assassination.

Out-of-office democrats are hardly ghosts in a Shakespearean sense, but they can serve a similar function. One day soon, probably long before Act 5, Republicans will be held to account for the evils they have brought to the American way of life.

It is often said words have consequences. Democrats will help voters remember "Lock her up!" was chanted at Donald Trump's rallies. "We will come after you and we will prosecute you" is a favorite phrase of Attorney General Pam Bondi. "Drill baby drill" will become an albatross around the necks of those who ruined the environment. "One big, beautiful bill" will become an anthem to remind voters of the Republican destruction of health care for millions of people.

Although lacking Shakespearean eloquence, Republican words and phrases will live after them. It is doubtful there will remain any good to be interred with the bones of their crumbling electoral kingdom.

In the end, Fortinbras, symbolizing strength, character, morality, duty, and high reputation is poised to take over the Danish kingdom, reversing the corruption, lies, betrayal and evil deeds of a false king. A worthy Mark Antony survives the tragedy of Julius Caesar to assume the rule of Rome. Restoration of legitimacy attends the ending of Macbeth.

Whether an analogous finality to the Trump regime happens is for a future act to reveal as our American tragedy plays out. It also depends on the quality of Trump's successors. We shall see.

Fighting Repression

Memories are dangerous. They invite comparisons to a past that will never be again, and possibly never was.

Coming of age during the John F. Kennedy years was glorified by the title of a book, *The Once and Future King*. We let ourselves believe knights of the round table, an image that implied fealty and dedication to a central purpose, were honorable, virtuous, and willing to fight for principles that transcended mere material existence. Richard Burton's rendition of a Lerner and Loewe song said it all:

> *A law was made a distant moon ago here:*
> *July and August cannot be too hot.*
> *And there's a legal limit to the snow here,*
> *in Camelot. ...*
> *In short, there's simply not*
> *A more congenial spot*
> *For happily-ever-aftering than here*
> *In Camelot.*

Of course, there were a few wrinkles in this story of benevolent rule by a progressive king who had his eye on creating a universe better than the one in which he lived. In the glades lurked the evil Mordred who threatened to bring the kingdom down. Beautiful Guinevere, who sang with the purest voice God's green earth could produce, was seduced by a young and virile Lancelot. Who could blame them for scumming to the delights of spring? And then there was Merlin, a kindly old magician who prophesied the future but could not alter the foreboding present.

In 1961, we were ebullient, delirious with the promises for a better future. It was a century when politician's speeches were scrutinized to be sure every word was true, not just to find one true word.

We chose to believe JFK had saved the world from a nuclear holocaust by facing down Khrushchev on the open seas. The Bay of Pigs disaster wasn't our fault—that terrible communist Fidel Castro got lucky! Only a small number of advisors were sent to help a southeast Asia country, Viet Nam. Nothing to worry about. "We," said Kennedy, "are going to send a man to the moon and bring him back safely, by the end of this decade."

Heady days, those were, that is until Kennedy was assassinated. It was left to Lyndon Johnson to land a man on the moon, usher in a period of government investment with the *Economic Opportunity Act*, pass the *1964 Civil Rights Act*, articulate and pass the *Great Society* programs, and, unfortunately, ignore Dwight D. Eisenhower's admonition to never attempt to fight a land war in Asia. Like Camelot, America's war in Asia ended with tragedy, disheartenment, millions dead, shame and destroyed dreams.

Make America Great Again is the new tablet of this land. Not poetic words, flowery speeches, or angelic songs, but dictums pursued under the banner of might makes right.

Laws with centuries of precedence are thrown out, ideals set in the Constitution of the United States are now tabu. Cancellation of *New Deal* programs are glorified as cost saving. Bribes and larceny are named the art of the deal, and transgressions against women are called consensual encounters. Mordred, it seems, was a knight ahead of his time:

Honesty is fatal, it should be taboo …
If charity means giving, I give it to you …
Fidelity is only for your mate …
It's not the earth the meek inherit,
It's the dirt …

Meanwhile, Democrats are lining up to see who gets to pull the Arthurian sword, Excalibur, from the rock.

Dueling for Grift

Alexander Hamilton's accomplishments were many before he was killed by Aaron Burr in a duel over a perceived slight to his honor. As one of the founding fathers of the United States, Hamilton was leader in the Revolutionary War, worked on drafting the Constitution and contributed to the Federalist Papers.

As Washington's Secretary of the Treasury, Hamilton established the national bank, the U.S. financial system, a debt repayment plan, a tax protocol, the U.S. Monetary System, mints, tariffs, and the Coast Guard. He believed that a strong central government was needed to engender a robust economic system. Hamilton's picture is on the U.S. $10 bill.

There is little similarity between Donald J. Trump and Alexander Hamilton except for coincidences of using in tariffs for financial gain. Hamilton believed in utilizing gold as a standard for backing up the value of money and tariffs as a mechanism for generating funds to support government expenditures and insuring   acceptance of American commerce. His intention was to strengthen and stabilize U. S. currency in order to instill confidence in the American economy among countries around the world.

Trump's regressive monetary policy appears to be directed toward an opposite goal—to weaken the dollar sufficiently to allow its replacement with crypto currencies. His plan will force the United States into bankruptcy, possibly having the intention of avoiding paying the national debt that his policies are doubling and tripling. His tariff war is aimed at making others, e.g. middle class American taxpayers, foot the tax bill for the richest oligarchs, not to speak of increasing his own wealth. His sham investments in phony currencies—bankrolled by duped MAGA followers—have engulfed his delusionary mind to the extent that he has even issued a 'coin' with his face on it.

Although Trump is yet to return to the gold standard as an instrument of monetary policy, his 'Goldfinger' fascination with the glitter is portrayed by gold faucets in personal bathrooms and as his theme for redecorating the oval office in the White House.

The United States is on the verge of accepting Trump's 'crypto mania' in the name of regulating the industry. Regardless of crypto's documented fraudulent history, senators argue that through legislation investors will be protected from scams and being cheated if laws allowing for open trading of cyber currencies are enacted.

It's part of a trend, such as legalizing drugs, ensuring guns for everyone, taking fluorides out of water, prohibiting inoculations as a first guard against childhood diseases, and abandoning the rule of law for perceived offenders and innocents alike. Grift is the name of Trump's day. Wouldn't a more appropriate acronym be 'gypto' instead of 'crypto'?

What have we become?

Credible observers report 14,000 babies and young children will die in the next 48 hours (end of May 2025) because Netanyahu's government will not allow humanitarian food into Gaza. We, of course, care intensely that our President, Donald J. Trump, whines in fear that he might not get his $400 million airplane gift from Qatar.

International war crimes agencies condemn the Israeli government for conducting genocide in Gaza. We, with great concern, wring our hands over the few undocumented migrants who may have received health benefits from our dwindling $2.9 trillion Social Security fund.

England, Canada, and some European countries promise to stop supporting the war machine if Israel continues to slaughter thousands women and children each month. We, in utmost sincerity, debate how many billions of dollars' worth of airplanes and bombs we can 'sell' to Israel each year.

The kill statistic for Gazan women and children, ignoring those uncounted souls buried under rubble or blasted into unrecognizable oblivion, reaches hundreds, maybe thousands, on any given day. We, those who are not sleeping, debate a 'big, beautiful bill' at one o'clock in the morning to shield our sensitive taxpayer sensibilities from the horrors of oligarchic grift.

Small Gazan children, holding shiny AID-provided pans, push and shove each other for the right to beg for another day's food. The smallest children risk being trampled under the feet of those slightly larger. We, while eating the desert at our evening meal, contemplate the effects of crypto technologies on the world's economies.

On the ground Gazan media workers' death counts reach levels higher than all previous wars combined. We, using our best literary acumen, reward reporters who uncover the latest celebrity 'tell-all' scandal.

Our Mother's Day is uncelebrated by the people of Gaza; all of the mothers and grandmothers are dead, dying or mourning the deaths of their children. We, as always, welcome the spring season with flowers and glory in the warmth of matronly appreciation.

Listen to the screams, and bombs, and cries and tell me, please tell me, this is not what have we have become?

Last Night's Nightmare

Ever since I was young, I've been plagued with dreams and nightmares. Most are insignificant, the product of over excitement or too much sugar candy. But last night's nightmare, and several that preceded it, have me worried.

It began a few years ago when I dreamed an unknown disease had begun to infect everybody I knew. At first, a few old people in a distant city I had lived in died in seemingly record time. The dream bothered me, but I didn't pay attention until a later nighttime disturbance implied the disease was expanding to where I now lived, taking lives of those closest to me. I woke with a sweat, looked around me in the night, and followed my wife's admonition to go back to sleep. I did.

A couple of nights later, the dream came again in the form of a nightmare. Dozens of people I knew were dying. Hundreds in every town and city were being carted away without even the grace of a funeral. Thousands in each state were showing up as casualties of the spreading disease. Doom sayers were projecting a death toll of millions! Worst of all, they said there was nothing we could do except wear cotton masks and pray. Our newly elected President claimed an inoculation of cleaning fluid would kill the virus. I woke up screaming; my wife soothed me back to sleep.

After several months of repeated nighttime terror, the nightmares morphed into bad dreams. The nightmare attenuation implied a different solution involving national quarantines and several billion dollars investment in developing and distributing vaccines and healing drugs that successfully combatted the effects of the disease. It had exploded into an international pandemic.

Although phantom skeptics poo-pooed the extreme care forced on us by a new and wiser President, my dreams became less dire, and I started to enjoy a full night's sleep. My wife was pleased not to be wakened by a hysterical man sleeping beside her. Then it happened again.

"What's wrong?" she almost shouted, her sleep interrupted by my screams.

"The nightmare has returned," I said, "this time it's worse than ever." I was sweating, panicked, disoriented, feeling extremely depressed.

"Okay. You're going to a social service therapist," she commanded me.

The recent replacement therapist was a kindly, middle aged woman who had heard uncountable stories before from distraught wives and frightened men. Over several sessions, she drew my anxieties out of my terrified subconsciousness.

"I thought the nightmare had gone away," I told her. "Then, last night, it returned more horrible than ever before."

"Tell me about it." She had placed me under hypnosis. "Don't worry, I am right here, and I will protect you," she said.

"The nightmare was terrible like before in a new setting. Somehow, the older President who saved us all was forced out of office, his VP voted down, and the evil one who told us to shoot Hilex into our veins took over."

"Yes," she soothed me, "that would be bad, but not so bad that you should have nightmares over it."

"I know," I said. "But it got worse, much worse."

184

"Oh. How could it get any worse?" she asked.

"In my bad dream, the nightmare President's first action was to release back into society thousands of rioters who sought to overthrow the government."

"That would not be good, but you could convince your subconscious that even though there are thousands of them, the rioters of your dream, there are millions of us to oppose them." She was trying to calm me with words. I was becoming animated in the throes of my hypnotic trance.

"No, no," I countered. "The dream got worse. The President appointed people to help him subvert the government himself. He surrounded himself with people who threatened to arrest, deport, and disenfranchise anyone they thought didn't like them."

"Oh, calm yourself," my therapist said. "They would never do that. There are laws against that sort of thing."

"I know, but I also dreamed that the Supreme Court said the President could not be held to account by those laws. Also, he can pardon any of his enablers who the courts try to restrain."

"Don't work yourself into a frenzy," she countered, now becoming a little worried that my behavior was becoming uncontrollable. "There are still judges who will refuse to be cowed."

"But I dreamed even they are being thrown in jail. Oh, god, this is the worst nightmare I've ever had!"

"Please calm down. You are still in a hypnotic state, and I can bring you back at any time. Use your mind to consider that the objects of your dreams, people in your imagined nightmare, are all external. You are internalizing fears and threats that are about others, not about you."

"It is about me!" I screamed. "Not only has he disbanded the courts, but he has commissioned a group of storm troopers to kidnap, arrest, and jail us, me included, just like Hitler did. They are called MAGA-ICE."

"I'm so sorry," she said, putting her arm around my shoulders to still my trembling.

"The worst part of my dream was being forced into a strait jacket, unable to move my arms and legs, sweating and trying to scream. I woke up tangled in a sheet with my pillow over my face. It was terrible."

She brought me out of my hypnotic state.

"I'm sorry, Mr. Weir. This therapy is not doing you any good. I cannot help you, but I cannot let you harm yourself or others either. These men will take you to a place where you won't harm anyone else or yourself."

The men, wearing caps with ICE written on them, placed handcuffs and leg irons on me, forced my head toward the ground, and took me to a waiting airport car.

Iron Doom

During the late 1940s, I was in the second and third grade in a small, four room rural school in northern Minnesota. We were told our lives were saved by taking the Sauk polio vaccine. We lined up in the lunch room and watched everyone else, hoping not to be the weak child who cried from the needle poke. Before we reached the door, we'd already recovered from the inoculation's pain and were happy to do nothing while waiting for the bell to ring signaling the end of our welcomed unscheduled recess.

For months we were lectured about what to do if the evil Chinese or terrible Russians decided to send an atomic bomb our way. We weren't told the United States had used bombs on two Japanese cities, immediately incinerating nearly 200,000 people. We weren't told that we had exploded several of these bombs in our southwestern desert and on remote Pacific Islands forcing evacuation of only a few native people. We weren't told America was already racing the Russians to construct a hydrogen bomb a thousand times more powerful than the atomic bombs that had destroyed Nagasaki and Hiroshima.

We were told to practice survival techniques in case the bad, bad Chinese and communist Russians decided to nuke us. Our small six and seven year old bodies were told to hide under our wooden desks even though several broke under the crush of careless adults who tried to sit on them. We were advised these desks would protect us from an atomic bomb attack.

The fallacy of that procedure soon dawned upon the wisest advisors the war department could field.

The next set of instructions informed our parents that they should build bomb shelters in the back yard. Many people used government-provided schematics and their own ingenuity to construct highly elaborate shelters to enable them to evade the worst effects of an atomic bomb attack. Presumably, they were adequately stocked with canned foods to last the 34 thousand years it took for the radiation levels to become safe again.

For some reason, it dawned on the masterminds of nuclear warfare that one's chances of survival were limited should such an event occur. This led to the next splendid defense theory, maximum deterrence. The wisest heads discovered that the only way thermonuclear war was survivable was not to have one. To even consider an exchange of nuclear bombs was mad.

MAD, 'mutually assured destruction,' became the gospel of the war planners. Certainly, they thought, the enemies' prospect of being burned to death if one made even the slightest move toward incinerating us would be enough to deter even the most adamant nuclear-age warriors from attacking first. (Years later, the 9-11 bombers showed the weakness of this theory.) This served the bomb makers well, because unless a nation had a bunch of bombs and missiles to deliver them, the MAD acronym didn't apply. Thus, we built an early warning system across Canada to the north and made more bombs that we would never use--first.

A defense based on scaring the enemy out of attacking wasn't too comforting, even though it worked for over fifty years. We already had assured ourselves that the enemy—USSR, China, and who knows what other sneaky devils, i.e. North Koreans, Iranians, or the Pakistanis, might get a bomb—was ruthless, powerful and God forbid, willing. We had to come up with a better defense.

Well, guess what? Just as the twenty-first century arrived, our only friend in the Middle East, Israel, found itself forced into a defense posture because of all of the hostile missiles that were headed its way. Initially, Israel tried to shield its population from lethal attacks by striking first, not with atomic weapons which they were thought to have and didn't rule out using, but with an unlimited arsenal of large and small conventional bombs procured from Israel's staunchest ally, the United States of America.

All too quickly, Israel is dropping more bombs on neighboring countries than were unleashed in all of the wars that proceeded it combined. Their leader, Benjamin Netanyahu, assures his Christian friends, successive Presidents of the United States, that Israel's surgically aimed bombs hit only active enemy targets. Killing of women and children and other non-combatants, is minimal, dubbed unfortunate collateral damage. Relieved, Democratic and Republican American politicians act assured. Billions of dollars' worth of bombs and delivery systems manufactured in the United States continue to be exported to our staunchest ally, Israel. Bomb, baby, bomb!

It doesn't work. The more bombs Israel drops on unsuspecting targets, the more enemy retaliation is attempted, supported by other nervous Islamic countries. Convinced that something more has to be done, Benjamin Netanyahu pursues a two-pronged strategy. The first prong is to imprison or destroy as

189

many perceived enemies as possible. When jails are filled, he resorts to killing. His current enemy, the hated Hamas, have infiltrated the people of Gaza. Together, Gaza has lost 55,000 souls to date. Each day another hundred women and children die, plus one or two Hamas warriors.

Bebe, as he is affectionately known by his American news supporter friends, will broach no dissent, and neither will his greatest advocate, Donald J. Trump. Speak up, you are an antisemite. Allow students to criticize, you are subject to your grants and contracts being rescinded. Speak loudly, you are branded an enemy of Americans and Israelis alike. Speak too loudly, you will get a visit from the FBI and/or ICE especially if your nationality isn't 'white.' Invite Bebe to speak to a joint session of Congress and you become a MAGA hero.

Okay, enough diatribe. Now I will get to the point! I started this essay with my six and seven year old self being told to hide under a desk. History has a way of repeating itself. To protect itself from missiles lobbed at 'ancient Palestine,' Israel with help from the United States has constructed an 'iron dome' to hide under. The ingenious defensive dome in reality consists of highly engineered 'counter' missiles that blow up incoming threats before they can reach an Israeli target.

It is important to understand that it is conventional missiles that are being blown up. Hamas, Lebanon, Yemen, and possibly Iran, together with other less nationalized enemies of Israel, don't have sophisticated weaponry sufficient to destroy Israel even though that is their stated goal. Thus, the concept of the Iron Dome is viable, so far, for Israel.

And it is working. One or two of the enemy missiles have landed on Israeli homes, but for the most part, no enormous damage has been done, except to Bebe's mind, who continues to follow a policy of exterminating anyone who doesn't speak Yiddish.

The lesson hasn't been lost on Donald J. Trump. He cannot live with Israel having an Iron Dome while he does not. Congress, he screams in the middle of the night, must appropriate a couple of trillion dollars so that an Iron Dome can be fitted over the continental United States. This must be done before Donald retires from the Presidency so help me God! Then, and only then, will we be safe from the horrors of foreign attack. (As a backup, Trump is sure to have considered that few intercontinental ballistic missiles carrying nuclear warheads may be blown up, but our unused bomb shelters left over from the 1950's can become a handy reserve security measure.)

A Senator from North Dakota is welcoming bringing the Iron Dome anti-missile missiles to his state, which already has a history of hosting silos filled with ballistic missiles. Best of all, this latest of defense strategies surely can be paid for from unneeded Social Security funds saved by the "big, beautiful bill."

Think of the future, forget the past. Nuclear war is not my first love but is guaranteed to be my last. That's a paraphrase from one of Elvis Presley's songs.

Your Check is in the Mail

I attended three of the Indivisible protests at the Veteran's Memorial Bridge between Fargo and Moorhead. I was assured that a rich oligarch would pay me for my time spent, as no real, honest, patriotic MAGA citizen was available for the work.

Including the time spent creating my meager protest sign, I spent in total ten and one half hours marching back and forth across the bridge. At North Dakota's minimum wage rate of $7;25 per hour, I calculate I should be paid $76.13. (Minnesota's minimum wage is set at $11.13 per hour, but I assume the lesser of the two applies, and I believe most of my time was spent on the North Dakota half of the bridge.)

In spite of the loss of 50% of your Tesla stock value, Elon, I know your check will be faithfully honored by the U.S. Treasury. Please send your remittance directly to my bank account. I will bill you weekly for future protest activities as they occur. Thank you, Elon, you are a wonderfully generous man.

Note: Elon Musk was quoted as saying the protesters were paid for agents of the Democratic Party. Donald Trump has made this allegation several times as well.

Speechless

I usually have something to say but after Trump's Memorial Day diatribe, I am left speechless. "...Sound and fury, signifying nothing" would be an acceptable mantra characterizing this President's speech were it not for the shame he casts on us all. Those who died so that others could live deserve better. From now on, Memorial Day silence would be more fitting from this man who knows no limit on insensitivity.

The Arc of History

The Covid 19 pandemic was defeated because a cadre of highly intelligent and dedicated scientists worked tirelessly to produce a vaccine and cure in record time. A newly elected democratic president utilized the power of his office to manufacture and distribute the remedy worldwide. President Biden overcame the skepticism and howls of head-in-the-sand MAGA Republicans to save the world from a disease potentially as lethal as the plagues of the middle ages that killed a third of the population of Europe.

Biden's achievements would not have happened had Donald Trump's attempt to overthrow the government succeeded. Even though seven million people worldwide died from Covid 19, hundreds of millions of others were saved from a gruesome death by President Biden's leadership.

Thanks and accolades are due to medical professionals, nurses and first responders, and insistent citizens who contributed to defeating Covid 19, but not one kudo is due to Donald Trump whose only advice was to inject a household disinfectant to kill the virus.

Republican revisionist history is attempting to diminish the success and valor of the Biden presidency and American democracy. Trumpism, MAGA, DOGE and ICE are implementing Project 2025 bent on destroying the institutions of truth in America.

Law, justice, science, medicine, business, education, environment, agriculture, and other foundations of knowledge are being systematically gutted of personnel and funding. Settled legal, medical, and scientific facts are being denied. Repositories of information, journals and news media, and books and libraries are being thrown out and/or defunded. Even grade schools for beginning learners are being closed or threatened with removal if they do not teach the gospel according to Trump. Each day one believes it couldn't get worse, and then it does.

Nevertheless, there are lessons to be learned from history. The first years of World War II were clouded by American losses on the battle fields of Europe and the Pacific, yet in the end perseverance and sacrifice won the war. The Cold War that promised a fiery end to much of the planet was negotiated to a stalemate with SALT treaties. Over a year passed with rising deaths from Covid 19 before even a glimmer of hope was given as progress toward a vaccine which ultimately conquered the virus.

It is not an overstatement to observe that the bubonic plagues of the Middle ages and Hitler's Nazism of the Twentieth Century were overcome by the inherent goodness of humanity. The current plague of Trump, MAGA and ICE will be defeated for the reason that good people choose to act. It is already happening.

Art as Metaphor

The grandfather stood holding the hand of a little girl who had only a few words in her vocabulary looking at a painting on the wall of a museum. Not far away stood the museum attendant, unobtrusively watching the patrons.

"Pretty," said the little girl. Her attention was soon diverted away from the abstract painting on the wall. She pulled her grandfather's hand toward another hanging.

They returned to the museum a year later to the same spot and gazed again at the painting on the wall.

"I remember this picture," she said. "We saw it last year."

"What do you think of it now?" the grandfather asked as the two of them gazed intently at the piece of art.

"It's still pretty," she said. "I like all of the colors and shapes. They make me feel happy."

The art excursion for that year ended when a bunch of rambunctious teenagers passed uttering boisterous one-word epithets about the crappy art in the museum. The uniformed attendant frowned at the teenagers and cautioned them to 'Keep it down.'

The next year the girl had grown several inches, but she still stood holding her grandfather's hand. Her hair was long, she had blue eyes, and she was talking a mile a minute.

"Oh, grandfather. Let's stop here at our painting again. This is the one I like best of all in the whole museum."

After viewing the painting for some time, the grandfather asked, "Why do you like this picture best of all?" They had seated themselves on a small, cushioned bench placed so that they could look one at a time at any of several of the paintings in the room.

"Well," she said, scrunching up her face in profound thought, "first of all, I like it because it is ours—the one we come to see every year."

Her grandfather gave her a little hug. That was why he liked the painting too.

"Secondly, it has different colors everywhere in it. It's like they are all living together in a picture, talking to each other in color language."

The grandfather was a little confused about the meaning of 'color language,' but the attendant who overheard the conversation acted as if it was a perfectly legitimate observation.

Again, the grandfather and young girl returned for a third time to the museum to view new and continuing installations. This time it was the girl, still a preteenager, who was patiently leading her grandfather from room to room, taking care not to tarry too long but also not to tire out her grandfather. His shoulders were not as square and erect as they had been in earlier years, and his steps were slightly unsteady.

"Let's sit here," the grandfather said, "and see if our picture is still using color language to speak to us."

The attendant was the same person as had occupied the station a year before, but he, too, was a little older with graying hair and lines in his forehead. He nodded knowledgeably to the girl with a smile that said he was glad to see them back.

"This year," the granddaughter began, "I see that the colors in the painting not only are talking to one another, but they are having a serious discussion about their world."

"That's interesting. What makes you think they're having a serious discussion?"

"See that open v-shape near the center? Its purpose is to tell the round listening shape facing it what's going on off to the side. Those short yellow, dark blue and green lines coming out of the v are color words that the round shape is hearing. It's serious because the color words are almost like angry sparks."

"Hmm. I never thought of it that way." The grandfather looked over to the attendant who was also examining the painting, this time through the eyes of the young girl.

"And those dark ominous shapes off to the side are waiting to challenge the colors in the center but they aren't quite strong enough yet."

"Do you think the bright colors will be able to hold back the dark invaders?" the grandfather asked, himself being drawn into his granddaughter's perceptions of the painting.

"I don't know, grandfather," she replied, "but next year we'll find out."

After thanking the attendant, they left the room and completed their museum journey, chattering between themselves about how lucky they were to be able to come back each year to a museum full of paintings that told stories with colors.

They didn't return the following year, but two years later the pair appeared at the museum doors. This time the grandfather was seated in a wheelchair being pushed by the girl, now a serious young person verging on womanhood. Access to the building was enabled through a side door that opened to an elevator used to bring heavy art objects to the gallery floors.

"Hello," greeted the attendant who was not at his usual station but recognized his visitors from earlier occasions. "We missed you last year. I'm glad to have you back." He began to lead them away from the room they usually visited.

"We'd like to start with the abstract picture we always view," the grandfather said.

"I'm sorry," the attendant responded apologetically. "Your painting is not available for viewing this year."

"Why not?" the grandfather asked, slightly perturbed at the attendant's deflection of his request.

"I'm sorry," he answered. "The abstract—the painting you always view each time you come—is out for repair."

"Repair!" the grandfather exclaimed. "Why does it have to be repaired? Paintings get old, but they don't fall apart." His two companions were saddened by the grandfather's observation.

The attendant decided the visitors deserved a fuller answer to the reason for the absent painting. He opened the door to the now empty gallery and ushered them inside.

"Your abstract hung in that space," he said pointing to an empty wall in front of the cushioned bench. "I was called away for a short time to take care of other business when unseen by anyone a thug with a knife slashed the painting."

"Oh, that's so terrible!" the granddaughter said.

"We believe he only meant to steal it, but when he heard me returning he chopped it up with his knife."

"How could anyone be so cruel and stupid?" she asked with a tear in her eye.

"For sure, it's was an evil thing to do," the attendant answered. "We'll need considerable time to put it back together. I promise it will be restored," he said.

She stared at the wall, reimaging the painting from her memory. "I can help," she said.

Together, grandfather, his granddaughter, and the museum attendant stared at the empty wall space where the painting had hung above a small brass nameplate. It was inscribed with two simple words, *American Democracy*.

Tall Grass

From the time the first Europeans landed on the shores of North America, developers sought to 'tame' the wilderness, abhorring the thought of living with it. The once plentiful forests said to hold an infinite number of trees that would last a thousand years were cut down in less than a third of that time. Rivers were straightened, dredged, damned, and drained in the march toward modernity. The Great Plains, a sea of grass and at one time millions of buffalo are now divided up into pristine sections with roads and highways ensuring access to every cultivated acre.

Small streams have been plowed under, and the fish that once lived there reduced by pesticides and herbicides to the distant memories. Grandfathers now ruminate about the 'good ole days' when there was a trout lurking in every stream's riffle, feeding under every overhanging bush, and hiding in the shadows of the banks.

Explorers marveled at the size of America, traveling west through the cattail dominated wetlands of Minnesota to the giant sequoia forests of California. Legends grew up around the exploits of Lewis and Clark, Kit Carson, Hugh Glass, and numerous 'mountain men' who overcame natural elements of ice, snow, drought, and starvation just to discover what was on the other side of the next hill.

Mythologies were built around real and imaginary exploits. Johnny Appleseed spread roots and cuttings across the landscape. Paul Bunyan felled the forests to create dimension lumber to build great cities. Annie Oakley could shoot out the eye of a carnival renegade at a hundred yards.

The genesis of national parks began when Ulysses S. Grant signed a law establishing Yellowstone as the world's first national park in 1872. John Muir took Theodore Roosevelt on a camping trip to Yosemite which resulted in a large tract of mountains, rivers, cliffs, and canyons being set aside for a park that came into existence in 1890. North and South Dakota's badlands were designated by President Roosevelt as a 'Monument' in 1939 and became a national park in 1978.

Roosevelt's Presidential Library is currently being built in Medora, a small North Dakota town located in the Theodore National Park. To date, the United States has 63 national parks and over 400 protected areas administered by the National Park Service.

Parks are under threat. Historically, ranchers, miners, urban developers, railroads, oil and gas prospectors and homesteaders have balked at the idea that property should be held in general for U.S. citizens. They would rather that lands be available to those whom they argue would rescue them from the wilds, 'improve' on what nature has provided.

It became part of American conquest to drive the natives from their homeland residency, relegated to token reservations. Sections were set aside for civic development and railroads. Occupied and unoccupied parcels became available for purchase by those who could afford them and handed down to their own descendants.

Hundreds of thousands of acres are now owned by a few mega-rich individuals, from Manhattan to the mountains and grasslands of Montana. In the never-ending quest for more, the captains of wealth lobby, bribe, influence, and elect leaders who will sustain their domination of everything, everywhere, all the time.

Now to the point of this essay. Theodore Roosevelt National Park and other North Dakota parks are continually under threat of encroachment by oil and gas developers. Development not only destroys the natural ambiance of the landscape but pollutes the environment with roads, debris, defacing scars, toxic materials and periodic release of chemicals and deadly effluents.

"Drill, baby, drill!" may have helped five North Dakota MAGA politicians gain and retain their legislative seats, but theirs is one of the most anti-America exploitation schemes promoted since the Europeans landed at Plymouth Rock.

Conservation, preservation, and environmental inviolability should be our state's guiding watchwords, not ruining air, forests, grasslands, and natural wonders that make North Dakota unique among states. Regressive politicians need to be reminded they are only one election away from legislative unemployment. It is not too early to think about replacing them, but it may soon be too late if the devastation of our environment is allowed to prevail.

Militarization

I stood alongside of thousands of Afghans watching a parade of soldiers, tanks and trucks, guns, and other apparats of war. It was the fall of 1966. The procession was organized as a celebration of King Zahir Shah's birthday.

My principled motivation for joining the Peace Corps was to escape becoming embroiled in the American war in Viet Nam. I elected to serve for two years, or as long as it would take to evade the clutches of my home town draft board.

Protests had become large events across America as were the casualty figures documenting wounded and dead on both sides. Sound pictures of helicopters flying over the jungle were accompanied by gruesome stories of sharpened homemade stakes, tunnels and viper pits meant to kill and maim unlucky young American soldiers.

Naively, I thought, I had limited my exposure to what I had come to regard as the Pentagon's final solution to every dispute in the world to 'back there' and 'thousands of miles away.' I hoped it couldn't reach me safely self-exiled to what I was told was the most illiterate, poorest, and medically backward country in the world.

It wasn't to be. On a daily basis, my English-as-a-second-language students during our unstructured conversation periods reminded me of what evils the American forces were doing in Asia. Their nebulous English vocabulary became surprisingly good when arguing their opposition of America's Viet Nam war, using words one might expect to find in a gruesome horror novel (These same words would be called boring and tame now.)

They—my students—identified with the Viet Cong. Ideas of saving the world for democracy were silly ideas of college intellectuals and war mongers who manufactured bullets and bombs. 'Only the rich,' they said, 'could afford to be free.' And so forth.

I stood waiting with my friend and guide Golam Haidar who himself had been a telegrapher in the Afghan army as the parade approached.

I expected a few smartly uniformed troops with rifles to be integrated among marching people from Afghanistan's over 30 ethnic groups dressed in colorful tribal costumes. Maybe a cart heaped with muskmelons, grapes, peaches, pistachios, Afghan nan, rice, and dozens of other exotic foods would pass by. Certainly, there would be displays of Afghanistan's world renowned carpets and rugs. Undoubtedly mounted horsemen displaying their expertise at buzkashi (a rather violent form of polo) would be presented to the crowds of thousands who lined the streets of Kabul.

Nope. It was a one hundred percent military parade, designed to show the world that Afghans were ready, willing, and able to fight for their King and country, for years if necessary. It also had the planned effect of reminding any dissidents that a force larger than them was ready to crush them should any insurrectionist thoughts occur. Some of those dissidents had become noisy a year before and paid dearly.

Afghanistan in 1966 was peaceful, friendly, verging on prosperity and anticipating remaining a free Islamic monarchy. The King's birthday celebration was never planned as the beginning of decades of war.

It started with dissention generated by the Israeli defeat of Egypt in the 1967 three day war. Within five years, Afghans were fighting the Russians who saw an opening for extending their totalitarian empire. Next, Muslim Shia and Sunni religious sects elected to use force to settle historic disputes.

A near victory of 'our special forces' assisted Northern Alliance was defeated by the Taliban. Unable to extricate ourselves from 'our form of democracy at all costs,' especially given the threat manifested by the Al Qaeda attack on 9/11, the United States adopted the Afghan religious dispute dubbed as an attempted communist takeover as its own war. It became 20 years of costly fighting in the mountains with no end in sight.

Only after a Republican president pledged to end the war by withdrawing most of the fighting troops was the United States able to terminate its Afghan adventure. Belatedly, during the following Democratic presidency, the remaining American forces were airlifted out with a chaotic exit from the military airport at Bagram. Countless casualties, exile of thousands of Afghans refugees, and worldwide condemnation of the American involvement became the war's legacy.

The Afghan war ended the way the Viet Nam war ended, in unforgettable humiliating dramatic fashion. Aircraft evacuated remaining American troops with desperate abandoned nationals hanging on the wheels of the planes, some falling to their deaths as the cameras recorded their demise.

It began with a parade, a celebration of the King's reign, and ended in tragedy for two countries, deaths of innumerable soldiers and civilians, and the destruction of democratic good will across the world.

Another parade, a congratulatory bow to a self-proclaimed would-be King of the United States and the world for President Donald J. Trump, will occur on June 14, 2025. By his own proclamation, it is to be a military parade on the streets of the American capital in Washington, D. C.

How will that parade end? Will it be the crowning fulfillment of a deranged but harmless foolish man who hasn't grown up, or will it be the end of American democracy? Will it be a show of American might that subscribes to rule under the law, or will it be the beginning of American military rule?

History records that military parades have been used as the impetus for armed takeover of governments. Is June 14, 2025, merely a continuation of the January 6, 2021, insurrection? What will the opposition be, a few kids and old people holding signs and parading on a bridge, or millions showing their right to oppose a deluded king of the world that his way is not our way?

Whatever happens, it will be interesting.

Note: It was interesting. The military parade on the National Mall to celebrate Donald J. Trump's birthday was reported by most news and commentator media observers to be a boring waste of $45 million plus. Even as a demonstration of America's military might it was shameful and dangerous. The United States Army and Airforce are much better trained, prepared and armed than was conveyed by Donald Trump's extravaganza.

On the other hand, the 'alternative' parades collectively referred to as No Kings Day events that occurred in over 2,000 communities across America were interesting. Citizens expressed their belief in real democracy while condemning the disrespect and illegality being done by the Trump-MAGA, DOGE, and ICE regime.

Champion Boxer

It took only a single punch for Elon Musk's five year old son to destroy the Musk-Trump co-presidency. Having administered the most famous sucker punch in history, the miniscule musketeer ended his father's takeover of the world and relegated him to casting epithets and earth shaking complaints via Tweet. The pain Elon must have endured to utter his final DOGE words! Boy, that kid must have a wicked southpaw.

Now, Donald J. Trump will have to go it alone. Of course, he will benefit from FOX referees and the corner encouragement that comes from Vance, Hegseth, Bondi, Rubio, and Noem. The congressional crowd of MAGA Republican cheerleaders will be with him assuming another five year old doesn't appear to administer a TKO from the sidelines.

Remember Mohammed Ali's 'float like a butterfly, sting line a bee. [Trump] can't duck what [Trump] can't see' (my paraphrase). Trump now has to be on the lookout for the likes of Rand Paul and Joni Ernst, not to mention fellow cult members Ted Cruz and Lindsey Graham. These aspirants may not be current contenders, but in the helter-skelter world of Republican politics, who can predict where the next punch will come from?

Ungrateful to the end, the elder Musk claimed his exit from the world of politics was because he "couldn't take it anymore!" Surely he was referring to some other thing besides the rough and tumble of the government contact sports.

Musk and his co-president Donald J. Trump have been uniquely successful in wiping out FEMA, cancelling membership in WHO, gutting USAID, firing employees of Social Security and the National Science Foundation, and destroying the American health care system (I do understand Robert F. Kennedy, Jr. deserves the majority of credit for ending health care as we know it.)

Ostensibly, Elon Musk withdrew from the arena in protest of Trump's "big, beautiful bill" that Republicans wish to vote into law as soon as a couple of recalcitrant senators can be reintegrated into the fold. Because the costs are so large—in Musk's words, a 'pork filled, disgusting abomination'—not only Musk but several senators own futures may be forfeited if the bill becomes law. Little do they care about millions of Americans who will lose their health care to pay for rich oligarch's new boats and fancy space ships. In this ring, pocket books count, but only if they belong to the boxing ring champions.

I used to think the outcome was fixed, or in modern terminology, rigged, but I'm not so confident any more when a five-year old's roundhouse punch can change the world. Hammer the gong for the next round! I can't wait.

Back and Forth

"Madness in great ones must not unwatched go." Shakespeare's line could not be more apropos. The co-Presidents are burning up the airwaves with their babyish slanders of one another.

By listening carefully to the barrage of insults being flung in both directions, one might occasionally hear a glimmer of truth. For example, Musk observed that the 'big, beautiful bill' penalized his electric cars while letting big oil, who he pointed out receive enormous taxpayer subsidies, continue with their usual exploitive privileged grants, set asides, depletion allowances, etc.

Trump, on the other hand, said Elon was having a meltdown, hinting that Musk's drug use facilitated his having to leave the White House. Back and forth, back and forth.

"It's time," said the prim and proper Musk, "to bring out the big bomb!" What is the big bomb? Oh, Trump was sweet with Jeffrey Epstein's pedophilic retreat in 1992.

So what's new, Elon? We've known about Trump's island visits and his 'parties' with Epstein ever since the latter offed or was offed in jail to keep his mouth shut. Donald was convicted of 34 sex crimes--there's no there, there, Elon. Move on.

Trump is dumbstruck by the affrontery of Elon's molestation criticism of him, but he might listen to Bill Gates who observed "The picture of the world's richest man killing the world's poorest children is not a pretty one."

Of course, The Donald cheers deep sixing USAID, bankrupting Medicare, and Medicaid, and providing Netanyahu with all the children's genocidal bombs he can possibly drop in Gaza. Meanwhile, Trump is making it impossible for anyone in some African countries to escape whatever harms local despots plan for their slaughter.

There was a hiatus in the fall of TESLA stock after Trump announced Elon was leaving his limelight position with DOGE. Neverthelss, the reduction of TESLA stock values took another nosedive with Trump's newest complaints, erasing another $150 billion from Elon's corporate finances. That move in this game of thrones occurred when 'the art of the deal' expert hinted he might divest the U.S. government of Musk companies. "Whoops, there goes another rubber tree plant." We have high hopes.

"Great ones..." implies qualities that might be endearing, but there is nothing endearing about these two courtyard fools who are wrecking our country. They must be 'watched' lest they do irreparable harm.

During my youth, Abby Hoffman (if I remember correctly) compared the American war machine to the antics of giant dinosaurs wagging their tails in the middle of a highly populated city. These relics of an earlier epoch were stupidly harmless, but their tails so massive, tall buildings could be wiped out with a single swat. Whole civilizations might be decimated were combatting monoliths to be unrestrained.

King Claudius, Hamlet's licentious and murderous stepfather, cautioned that 'madness in great ones should not unwatched go.' In our modern context, watching means taking care to prohibit these evil actors from further destroying American democracy through their infantile daily spats with one another. June 14, 2025, is No Kings Day with protests planned for everywhere. Appropriate, don't you think?

Just Say No

The June 14 No Kings Day protests promise to be the largest in United States history. Hundreds of thousands, perhaps millions, of Americans will take to the streets to exhibit their rejection of the Trump, MAGA, DOGE, ICE, and congressional Republican destruction of democracy.

There is nearly universal agreement among the citizens of America who are saying 'NO!' to the would-be king that his days of unopposed tyranny are over. Respectable news outlets report that demonstrations are planned at over 1,500 sites in every state and province to express the irritation, distrust, denunciation, disapproval, anger, and condemnation of Trumpism.

The crowds of protesters will be carrying signs, wearing costumes, exhibiting phrases, and speaking their minds about what is happening to our country. Some will claim guiltlessness by exclaiming "I didn't vote for this SOB!" and "This is not what was supposed to happen."

Regardless of the intended message, the proponents will be individually correct in their assertions but as members of the American electoral class, wrong.

I, too, voted for the candidate from the other party, the Democratic Party. I voted for a person who demonstrated knowledge, intelligence, grace, honor, patriotism, strength, and willingness to become a President of the United States of whom I could be proud. I voted for a person I knew would make me feel safer, and whom I would trust with my daughter's and her daughter's future. I voted for compassion and decency in American political life.

214

But make no mistake, I voted for President of the United States because I believe in our system of government, and I trust the people of America. The people of America will do the right thing, even if it means to admit we have made a mistake and must correct it. Redress is written into the founding documents of our nation.

WE are Americans. WE are the people who put Donald Trump and his MAGA acolytes and yes men and women into office. It is OUR fault they are there, and if WE do not correct our error, WE will have earned any maltreatment he and his cadre of misfits bring to us.

The Supreme Court, the Congress of the United States, complaisant governors, like-minded sheriffs, and other law enforcement officers, (and almost no judges) are not to be excused. They occupy positions of power and have sworn an oath to support and protect the Constitution of the United States. Most have violated their oath of office.

Those in elective positions will have the SHAME of losing their jobs not because they stood up to evil but because they did not. They will be held to election account. Accountability for others will be SHAME, in the eyes of their children, friends and colleagues. It will be enough. It will follow them the rest of their lives.

This essay began with its title, "Just Say No." Nancy Reagan made the phrase famous by advocating its use when confronting the scourge of illegal drugs.

'Just Say No' is not a bad admonition. It takes a lot of strength to just say no and act accordingly. To some, saying no may mean throwing rocks, burning cars, spraying graffiti, hurtling insults, and blocking traffic. There are other more incendiary activities that could be interpreted as saying no that I choose not to name.

Those methods of saying no are not an answer to the MAGA activities they are meant to redress. Violence begets violence. Donald Trump and his people are losers; they are on their way out. Adopting their insane behaviors is not a remedy for our needs.

Civil disobedience can be administered in a non-violent manner. Mahatma Ghandi, Martin Luther King, Cesar Chavez, and millions of lesser known people have successfully advocated non-violent peaceful actions to advance their causes. Adopting non-violence as a mantra for the resistance movement does not mean acquiescence or giving in. It means being smarter than they are.

June 14, 2025, promises to be an extraordinary day in the annals of American history. If we can 'keep our heads while all others are losing theirs,' it will be a happy day as well. Please, be smart, be safe, and be careful. Just say no.

Are You Listening?

Recently, a democratic political advisor said, "The bottom line is President Trump..." and went on to suggest Trump should be the primary focus of the Democratic Party's future efforts. I disagree. Trump is a 'has-been', a weak old obese man who is becoming more senile and erratic each day. His reckoning will be handled by his god.

The Democratic Party, and like-minded Americans who truly desire a better future for their children and nation, should focus their efforts on 1) defining themselves in a way that is good for the country, not as a reaction against Trump and his acolytes, and 2) defeating Republicans, not to ascend themselves into high office but to rescue America from the injustice that Republicans are perpetrating on a daily basis.

The politics of attack and destroy, of hate and divide, and of greed and theft are those of a losing campaign. Especially since America will be emerging from an internal war of oligarchs against the people over the next two and four years, democrats need to present the achievable promise of a better future, not merely a reaction to the past.

We, the protestors of No Kings Day, are sending a message. Will the Democratic Party take notice?

Strawberry Fields Forever

Picking strawberries is backbreaking, stoop labor usually performed by temporary immigrant laborers who are paid low wages for combing the fields. Strawberries don't ripen all at once, so each row has to be repeatedly tended, sometimes two or three times in a season. The laborers work in the hot sun wearing as little clothing as diffidence will allow.

This day, one could see the green rows stretching forever. Each row was neatly spaced to allow mechanical pesticide implements and cultivators to pass without harming the fruit. Well protected foremen and crop duster pilots use implements and airplanes to apply poisons to kill bugs and ward off any birds that might choose to eat a colorful fruit. One commonly used pesticide is malathion, chemically classified by the International Agency for Research as a 'probable human carcinogen.'

An iPhone photographed three people racing down the rows, one slightly in front of the others. Were they smaller figures, one would suspect young children were playing among the strawberries while their parents worked.

Not so! Two ICE intruders were attempting to arrest a field worker whom they claimed was an undocumented immigrant. As he sped away, they shouted for him to stop, but he didn't. He had heard of the 'disappeared,' the 'kidnapped,' the 'incarcerated,' the 'strangled and beaten and starved,' the 'missing fathers and mothers and children' forcibly removed from American soil. He knew if he was caught he might spend the rest of his life in a foreign prison, forgotten among the thousands of other apprehended and deported migrant workers who had become the subjects of ICE operations.

Now, the apprehensions are happening across the United States. With nebulous legal backing, Tom Homan, Pam Bondi, and Donald Trump are terrorizing field workers, carwash attendants, sick children, expectant mothers, grandparents, husbands, and anyone who doesn't have the same skin color as they do.

Legal aid and courts are fighting back. Kilmar Abrego Garcia has been returned to the United States to face trumped up charges. The Turkish graduate student snatched off the sidewalks of Tufts University, falsely claimed to be a Palestinian, was freed after six weeks of imprisonment. A high school student, Marcelo Gomes da Silva, brought to the United States when he was seven years old and detained by ICE for overstaying his visa has received the backing of his town.

While a few highly publicized victims of ICE are being released, thousands of others are held in American and foreign prisons, unidentified and unable to contact a lawyer, clergyman or even a family member. The few returned victims of ICE are met with joy and relief from advocates who feel relief that their humanitarian efforts were rewarded.

Don't for one minute believe it! It's a cruel joke, a lie meant to lull a protesting public into false security and lethargy. While three or four first-grabbed people are temporarily freed, hundreds and thousands of others are taken from their homes, streets, towns, and cities each day.

ICE's obscene arrests continue, and they must be stopped. The real menace to America, the real criminals, are not the 'not white' illegal and undocumented workers and relatives. The real culprits are Donald J. Trump, Pam Bondi, and Tom Homan, and as many ICE operatives as someday can be identified.

Fear of future accountability is the reason why the ICE operatives wear masks. Confidence in being pardoned by Trump is the reason why Bondi and Homan don't wear masks. They are the law breakers, the violators of the Constitution of the United States. They should be arrested, tried, and sent to the same prisons they use for migrants.

Let me take you down

'Cause I'm going to strawberry fields

Nothing is real

And nothing to get hung about

Strawberry fields forever…

--McCartney/Lennon lyrics

Towering Mushroom Clouds

Amanita phalloides also known as the 'death cap' mushroom. When ingested, it produces seizures, coma and other stunning attendant symptoms ending in death for humans. Historical literature reflects it was a favorite ingredient used to cause the death of kings and other unlucky 'bystander' human beings. In appearance, it looks common, inviting and manageable. It isn't.

As the world edges closer to the use of nuclear weapons—conveniently recognizable by their towering mushroom clouds—it might be worth remembering how a now-decommissioned antique World War II prop plane named the Enola Gay managed to sneak through Japanese defenses to take out Hiroshima and Nagasaki, immediately incinerating hundreds of thousands of people in a flash. Many of those who survived the initial burst died from 'seizures, coma and other stunning attendant symptoms'.

Considered a master stroke by its proponents, the only use of atomic weapons still is a ghoulish blight on the conscience of humanity. But those without consciences, those who only saw magnificence in devastating destruction, lusted after the bomb. They constructed a rationale for producing more and more, proliferated acquisition and stockpiles, and proudly claimed nuclear superiority. Superiority meant (and still means) they could unleash their bombs at an antagonist ten seconds after that opponent had launched certain death and agony at them, guaranteeing incalculable destruction.

So, North American, European, Middle Eastern and Asian countries have the Bomb. These countries are ruled by crazed politicians who have phantasies of controlling the world. All of them are in the golden years of their lives, yearning to leave a lasting legacy. What will it be?

Peace, Not War

Well, it has arrived, *No Kings Day*. Between 1,500 and 2,000 cities, towns, villages, and multitudes of single individuals standing at the end of their driveways with protest signs will tell MAGA, ICE, DOGE and like-minded destroyers of the American way of life that their day is over.

My vigil will take place in Fargo because I want to support the rejection of Trump acolytes who claim to represent North Dakota's values and people. In my mind, they don't. They represent selfishness, vainness, and greed. They represent exploitation of the environment, subjugation of working people, indifference to the rule of law, and racist xenophobia of their ruling class.

But more so, I want my presence to mean a better day for North Dakota and America is coming. Americans are a 'can do' people. When we address problems, we solve them. When we see wrongs, we right them. When we confront evils, we defeat them.

And when we make a mistake, we correct it. Electing the MAGA Republicans was a horrible mistake, but it can be corrected. June 14, 2025, is a moment toward making what is wrong in our politics right again. Nationally and internationally, countries of the world are moving toward global war again. It doesn't have to be—"All we are saying is give peace a chance."

Standing Up 6/14/2025

What I saw was the best of Fargo citizenry and surrounding communities standing up for integrity, decency and justice. I was both humbled and proud to be among such good people.

Note: Written after attending a protest rally at the Fargo Civic Center on 6/14/2025.

Mourning for FEMA

One reads the national news and frowns to learn FEMA is on the Republican-Trump-DOGE target list for extinction or at least is a candidate for substantial reduction. 'Terrible,' I think, 'that an agency that often provides first responder help to disaster victims when they need it most should have its workforce and funding cut.' I'm thankful such calamity has not happened to me or my community, living safely up in northern Minnesota as we do. Then it does!

Last night, a tornado or straight line 106 mph wind called a derecho moved through eastern North Dakota killing three people, and into Minnesota where it downed thousands of trees, ripped roofs off buildings, tipped over cars and trucks, and damaged buildings and stores in the city of Bemidji. Other tornadoes, 14 by first count, ravaged other parts of Minnesota. Initial reports tell of impassible roads, downed electricity lines, damage to transmitting centers, and possible blackout for the next three days. One knowledgeable damage assessment person said it may be weeks before the destruction will be totally cleaned up.

Fortunately, my property suffered only a little damage that I can solve with a chainsaw and a complaisant insurance adjuster. But Beltrami county and Bemidji are among the poorest in the state. Even with homeowner insurance, major financial outlays will be necessary for some people. Thousands of area residents who are less fortunate than I will need FEMA-type assistance. Will it be forthcoming? We shall see.

Note: Written 6/21/2025 following Donald J. Trump's fifth full month in office.

Do You Feel Better Now?

Regardless of the 'rights' and 'wrongs' of American and Israeli bombers over Iran, the question remains, 'Do you feel better now?" Has the entry of your country into its fifth major war in the Middle East in the past three decades reduced your apprehensions and made you happier?

To recap, a proxy war opposing the Russians in Afghanistan, another twenty years of direct Afghan engagement, two wars in Iraq, strikes against Yemen and other opposition 'hideouts', and continual munitions support to Israel for the extermination of Hamas together with thousands of Palestinians—mostly women, children, and bed-ridden hospital patients--as collateral damage about sums it up. (We did manage to take out Osama bin Lauden, a Saudi Arabian mastermind of evil, but we do not go to war with the Saudis!)

Yesterday, the United States once again committed itself by direct intervention in Israel's war with anyone in the Middle East whom it doesn't like. Iran's 'weapons of mass destruction' targets were obliterated, according to our president, in three locations. We are assured that this was a 'one-off', a surgical strike meant only to degrade Iran's capability for building a nuclear bomb, not to accomplish regime change or any other military objective. Whatever other objectives remain will be settled by the Israelis who are systematically reducing Omar Khayyam's Persia to ashes.

The United States builds the bombs, provides the bombs, and now delivers the bombs that maintain the seemingly perpetual internecine conflicts in the Middle East. Is this why you willingly pay your taxes, support autocratic rulers, deport Hispanic farm workers, quadruple the national debt, cancel social safety net programs, etc. Does it make you happy? Do you feel better now?

Postscript

The June 14, 2025, *No Kings Day* protests estimated to have involved several millions of people took place in over 2,000 cities and communities in all fifty states. With one exception, all were peaceful. The only significant violence occurred in Brooklyn Park, Minnesota, where a state democratic legislative leader and her husband were assassinated, and another state democratic legislator and his wife were gravely wounded in a separate attempted assassination.

It is uncertain whether the Minnesota assaults were related to *No Kings Day*. Police discovered a list of several prominent democratic state and federal politicians who may have been additional targets of the killer. Investigators also discovered a brochure about the *No Kings Day* protest, but (as of this writing) no motive has been attributed to the one perpetrator who has been identified and although apprehended has not made a clarifying public statement.

The End (for now)

About the Author

Ivan Lee Weir was raised on a small farm among the lakes and forests of northern Minnesota. Besides fishing, hunting, and trapping, his early years were spent caring for animals, wrestling hay bales, and milking cows by hand morning and night. After elementary and high school, he earned bachelor's and master's degrees at a local college. Following two years in the Peace Corps, he obtained a Ph.D. in Sociology from a western university that enabled him to pursue a career in research administration. He began authoring books after he retired from academia. Four of his books are novels written after he was 80 years old.

His first novel, *Murder at Coffee Pot Landing*, takes place in present time on the Mississippi river near Bemidji, Ivan's home town. *The River Walk Child* is the second of two fictional novels featuring Andrea Stratham and Soraya Chandrisi as central characters. The action of *The River Walk Child* involves solving an international conspiracy of art thefts. A third novel, *Bison River Madam*, is set in an imaginary town called Bison River, Minnesota, in 1937. The town is located near Comstock, Minnesota where the author's ancestors settled in the nineteenth century. Weir's other novel, *The Phantom Djinn*, is set in Afghanistan harking back to the author's 1966-7 Peace Corps experience.

Other books Dr. Weir has written includes a coffee table book about his great grandfather's bookplate engraving collection. Another is a historical drama about a seventeenth century ancestor, Michael Blackburne, who fought on the side of the Royalists to defend Pontefract Castle. He has also authored a book of autobiographical sketches called *Stories for My Daughter*.

Ivan Lee Weir currently lives in Fargo, North Dakota with his artist wife, Marjorie Schlossman, and their dog, Decaf. Together, they have a blended family of eight adult children and a growing number of grandchildren.

Made in the USA
Monee, IL
11 July 2025

20814994R00134